Mission MBA

Mission MBA

Rajiv R. Thakur

PRABHAT
PAPERBACKS

Published by
PRABHAT PAPERBACKS
4/19 Asaf Ali Road,
New Delhi-110 002 (INDIA)
e-mail: prabhatbooks@gmail.com

ISBN 978-93-5266-345-3
MISSION MBA
by Rajiv R. Thakur

Edition
First, 2017

Price
₹ 200.00 (Rupees Two Hundred only)'

Printed at
R-Tech Offset Printers, Delhi

Dedicated to
Bhargavi
Ritu
Godawari
Ishwar

Prologue

Padmasri
Dr. Pritam Singh
Ex-Director,
IIM Lucknow
Ex-Director,
MDI Gurgaon
Ex-D.G.
IMI New Delhi

After going through 'Mission MBA', I found this book to be highly useful for millions of youth of this country for whom MBA and its related career is a dream. It is a contemporary book for the students who join the MBA programme but hardly know what to look for during the two valuable years of the completion of programme. The students will find 'Mission MBA' a great guide for themselves.

This book is a powerful symbiosis of thought and action, unlike most of the books which focus on the thought aspects alone and neglect the action part. The author has elucidated all the nuances associated with the MBA, right from enrolment in the course to course curriculum, teaching-learning process, personality development, preparation for placement and importance of self-values. Another good aspect that I found in this book is the experts' opinion from different sections of the society which has been presented as a separate section apart from the author's own opinion and experiences. I must also appreciate the author for his language which flows like the rhythm of a flowing river.

I firmly believe that details explained in the book will be highly useful for students to develop a career in management and make them successful. Apart from students, this book would be useful for parents, guardians and faculty also. Overall, I can say with confidence that 'Mission MBA' has spared no effort in attaining its milestone.

I have known Dr. Rajiv R. Thakur, the author of the book, for more than a decade now, both in his role as a Professor and Director in different institutions and I have no hesitation in saying that whatever role he worked, he has brought about a positive and significant difference and has left behind a distinctive mark of success. I find in him every quality of a successful practising leader. I congratulate Dr. Rajiv R. Thakur, for his efforts which will directly benefit a large section of society. I further wish him all success in life.

(Padmasri Dr. Pritam Singh)

Preface

From tenth class onwards, there are many possibilities to choose a certain career, however it is very tedious and difficult task to find a certain and right direction. Due to lack of right information or laxity on part of students and parents it becomes difficult to decide what is to be done or not to be done after tenth class and same dilemma continues till the selection of a career. Even if one is able to decide a career and course related to it, then also dilemmas like how to succeed in that course and what is expected from a student while doing that course keep haunting students and they become a barrier in their success. Millions of students face this problem especially in cities and places where there is a severe lack of awareness and where very few knowledgeable and experienced people are there to guidethem in right direction. Same dilemma is faced in the families where elders, parents are unable to guide students due to limitation of their own knowledge. In my experience of over two decades in industry and educational institutions, I have seen many students struggling with this problem. I have seen many students who couldn't succeed in spite of having capability and potential to reach the peaks due to lack of right information and right guidance.

In this perspective, I realized from my experience why not right information is made available in the form of a book related to the courses and careers and all their relevant aspects to millions of students and their parents/guardians.

In doing so, I realized it was almost impossible to include all the streams and all type of careers in a single book. Thus, I have tried to throw light on problems and dilemmas faced by students in tenth and twelfth classes and those focusing on MBA course and management career.

Due to my association of over one decade with management institutions, I have got opportunity to see closely and realize difficulties faced by the students and their parents in choosing management career, management institutions, nomination process, nuances of management courses and getting placement after successful completion of the course. I have attempted in this book that, right information and right guidance reaches to students and parents on all above aspects of management career. Following points have been basically discussed in the book which will be considerably significant for the readers -

1. Necessary thinking in a family in context of current social and economic system and environment. Emphasis on need for education and skills.
2. Different opportunities available from tenth to twelfth classes and right guidance for choosing a desired direction for self from among these opportunities.
3. Growing influence of management career and details of contribution of MBA course in its success.
4. Introduction to the system of management courses and prospects in the country.
5. Nomination process in the management institution and necessary preparation for admission.
6. Guidelines on how to choose a right management institution
7. Introduction to the management course and all nuances of the course so that students can complete the course successfully.
8. Importance of summer internship and its process.

9. How to develop a holistic personality during the course so as to ensure credibility in the industry.
10. Information about placement process and necessary preparation for success in the same.

On the above points, on one side author has put forward his own views and experiences, on the other side, he has included opinion of selected experienced experts of the country. These experts have great expertise in different sectors of industry and education, and their experience and views will be very valuable and beneficial to the readers.

In addition to these important points, some useful information has been included at the end of the bookso as to benefit readers and develop their interest and tendency towards more information.

Apart from students and parents, this book would prove to be very useful for coaching institutions, under graduate colleges and plus two schools, especially in small towns where there is lack of information and experience even today. This book will be useful to both section of students one who want to opt for management career or the other section who are currently in 12th or under graduation courses and have to decide their path.

I am very delighted to dedicate this book to the readers, in which I am able to share in brief my views and experiences on all aspects of these highly useful topics. I believe that all readers will feel benefited from these discussions. It should be considered as a small gift from my side to the society.

□

Acknowledgements

'*Mission MBA'* is fruit of divine inspiration, and from bottom of my heart I want to express my gratitude and am subservient to the God for his blessings in the form of this book as *"prasadam"*. From my little achievements in the life so far, I could also return back something to society, this divine inspiration keep pinching my conscience and pamper me to do something in this direction and it is the result of this inspiration that this little book containing experiences of my life is presented before the readers and will surely benefit them.

My parents, family, daughter and wife have contributed quite significantly in this attempt, and they have always inspired me to do some such positive works. My wife Ritu has particularly enforced me to do something better as a critic in her own style and has provided her full support for the same. Apart from my family, some other highly valuable personalities associated with my life have inspired me through their intimate gestures and I express my gratitude to them. My gratitude to all my friends, and relatives! Inspiration from my colleagues, students, young ones and elders at workplace has been behind this book and I have narrated in this work, experiences gained while working with them. I acclaim the contribution of all expert friends who provided their valuable time and inputs for inclusion in this book. I would like to thank Mr. Jitender Sharma, my ex-colleague for all his timely help ever.

From the bottom of my heart I would like to thank Padmshri Dr. Pritam Singh, Ex-Director IIM Lucknow, MDI Gurgaon, Ex-D.G. IMI New Delhi for his valuable suggestions for the further improvement of the contents in the book. Not only he read through the entire manuscript but also blessed the author with his words of wisdon in writing 'Prologue' of the book.

Finally, I cannot end my acknowledgements without greeting and thanking Mr. Prabhat, publisher of Prabhat Prakashan, who not only agreed for publication of this book but carry out all works related to this publication very quickly. I would like to especially praise his simple and sober personality. May God bless him with great success! I would like to thank every member of the publishing company. Without their hard work this goal could not be achieved.

I sincerely hope that this book, Mission MBA, which is result of divine and noble souls' inspiration would be surely acclaimed by you.

— **Dr. Rajiv R. Thakur**

□

Contents

1

Education-skill and Family system

In the present social and economic situation, it is only education and skill of a person that form the basis of his existence. A person can be relevant in any walk of society only if he has a definite and unique skill and it is this skill which is the foundation of his life. In present-day knowledge-based economy, whether it is agricultural sector, manufacturing or the services sector or any other sector, there is a pressing need of relevant skill, practical knowledge and information apart from labor. Take the agricultural sector for example – today's farmer needs modern farming techniques and scientific agricultural practices to be successful in the agricultural sector. Detailed information about soil texture and profile, irrigation techniques, fertilizers, seeds and sowing, conservation and storage and the new information related to trade of agricultural produce in the market are essential for success and good reward for labor. The youth must abreast themselves with the new and advanced skills and education related to the agricultural sector. The age of information technology has made it easier to gather and process information about education and skill. On the other hand, it has also become very essential for them to be compiled for people. For the future generations and posterity especially the youth this situation is prevalent in almost all fields. They do need education, information and relevant skills to succeed in their respective areas of specialization.

In light of the importance of education and skill, it will be appropriate to say that every family and section of the society must be committed to its cause, the reason being the fact that the survival, success and prosperity of every individual, every family and every society hinges on these factors in today's age of knowledge. Thus, it becomes desirable that each family provide its members a suitable and conducive environment which can facilitate kids as well as young adults to focus on gathering knowledge and skill and also to understand their importance in their lives. For this to happen, first and foremost the family members and relatives must take the initiative and help in building an environment that promotes education and also stimulates the urge to learn. The children and young people in the house should be encouraged in the pursuit of excellence in education and the resources and necessary help should also be ensured. The inclination of children towards education is based on the level of commitment of the family towards education. Behind a successful student there is a committed and supportive family and devoted parents more often than not.

It is important for children in every family to have a dream and a goal in life. This dream shapes up their future and gives direction and purpose to the efforts of parents and brings their resources into relevance. Some rare examples include a father who helped his daughter achieve the goal to become a chartered accountant on the basis of his earnings from being an auto driver, a lot many instances of parents putting up a commendable display of selflessness and sacrificing every bit of their comfort to help their children scale unprecedented heights and achieve prestigious posts like doctors, engineers, I.A.S., magistrate, etc. These dreams were realized only when the parents or guardians saw a dream and to realize that dream they made a conducive learning environment at home and rationalized the use of resources that were limited, towards the fruitful realization of the dream. All families need this commitment and sacrifice regardless of their affluence because every family has some dreams and only these resolutions can help achieve them.

To achieve the goal, it is of utmost importance that the parents educate their children in a school-based educational structure as it helps to set a good solid foundation. To ensure good schooling, a good school must be selected. A good school must ensure ample opportunities for allround growth and development in a field of the choice of the child be it sports, music, writing, debate, quiz, etc. It helps growth of children in their field of interest apart from the emphasis put on practical knowledge associated with the knowledge being imparted in school. It is a common occurrence that parents are often casual about choosing a good school for their child. The proximity and flamboyance of the school and its brand image are often reason enough for parents to fall for it which should not be the case. Ideally, the ambience and environment, the structure of education, opportunities for children, teacher attention on students and the overall level of academic result should be the criteria for selecting a school. Schooling should be complemented by an excellent learning environment at home which must be facilitated by parents. Children should get a learning and studying environment at home also. This is very essential. Apart from studies in school, they should be encouraged to study their favorite subjects as per their interest. They should also be taught to gather information from websites on the Internet. Sports and games should be introduced as part of a daily routine and they should be allowed to take up a sport or even a hobby on the basis of their interest. These small things are necessary for the future career aspirations of a child.

In my own experience, when these things are taken into proper consideration, the results have been generally very positive and on the contrary when parents have taken things a little easily the children have had to face an uncertain and directionless future, due to which they have been forced to struggle a lot more. Apart from school if parents also do not give due attention to the issue then a negative effect is often seen on the kids. An irregular self-study pattern at home, lack of a regular routine, too much of gameplay, wastage of precious time with friends and all other things tend to have a negative effect on the steady growth of a child. Parents should be always aware of what their children are being taught in school. A regular assessment of the child's progress is also very essential for the evaluation of his development. Whenever there are deficiencies, they should be addressed in collaboration with the child and in case of a good quality proper credit should also be given to the child as it is necessary to promote good behavior. It has been observed that many parents keep the children involved in household activities which ultimately hampers the children only. Irregular school attendance, negligence towards studies at home and wastage of precious time in useless activities renders the child directionless and disoriented in the same measure as spending too much time in playing with friends. Apart from this, some parents create too much of a religious and social bend in their children which adversely affects their daily routine and does not allow them to stick to and follow a timetable. In my opinion, if children can take care of their own responsibilities and improve the facets of their personality and life then this is their biggest responsibility.

Looking around I can see many families whose examples have been nothing short of exemplary. Here the parents have virtually and literally sacrificed their entire lives for the children. Their reason of existence is dedicated to the well-being and welfare of their kids in all possible ways. Their time is devoted to kids apart from occupation. From studies to sports to entertainment, it is the parents who have been running from pillar to post to help the children feel safe and secure and wanted. Assistance in studies, solving their issues, spending quality time in evenings and during a holiday, watching films and television shows for entertainment, discussing national and international news, keeping children well informed, discussing family issues are all part and parcel of an ideally united and aware family.

The span of time that lies between the tenth and twelfth is very crucial for both kids and parents. They play the pivotal role in shaping their children's future in this period. This is a responsibility all should look to carry with honesty. College studies or further education should see more freedom apart from usual care. More freedom means leaving certain things to the taste and personality of the child as it helps him evolve and develop self-confidence and free thinking. These are essential for a happy and successful life. A child raised in an overprotective environment faces multiple challenges in living a fulfilling life because such kids are often seen as unhappy, anxious and unsure individuals and they are generally incapable to decide for themselves. I would like to warn here against the ill-effects of too much unsupervised freedom because this is the age when most of the youth gets misled and loses its way which ultimately culminates in disappointment and dejection for the family as a whole. The seeds of good habits and a strong moral set sown in the school days and the all-round raising of the child bear fruit in college days when the child understands his responsibilities in making a successful career as a fully capable and sincere youth. Apart from this his personality and character develop organically and seamlessly which is always a matter of extreme pride and satisfaction for the parents, guardians, family as well as the society. Such endeavors should be encouraged and promoted in every household.

□

2

Career Choice for Youth

As I recall period of last few decades, I realize that chances of getting jobs or career prospects for young people in the country were severely limited as compared to present days. Though after liberalization era in early nineties, new opportunities were generated in industries and especially private sectors, these were primarily limited in the traditional sectors only. Employment and career opportunities for youth were offered by government and public sector companies like SAIL, Indian Oil, N.T.P.C, Coal India, Railways, banks and L.I.C. to name a few. In addition, few more career options were open in professions like medical, engineering, C.A., C.S., management and legal but their numbers and scope were much limited than today. Starting one's own business was other available option but private start-ups were not so popular those days. The preferred opportunities and professions were government jobs, banking, doctors or engineers and it was evident from the fact that parents looked for grooms primarily from these professions only for marrying their daughters. Since the decade of 1990s when liberalization and globalization policies were introduced in India, the economy of the country has changed progressively and in accordance there is a shift in the job and career opportunities also. On one hand, opportunities in decades' old traditional sectors remained open, on the other hand with opening of private sector and arrival of multinationals, many new opportunities in these sectors opened up and demand for professions like engineering, management, banking, insurance, medical, C.A., and C.S., etc. grew multifold than earlier. There is a fast rise in new economic sectors like I.T., Research and Development, consulting, hospitality, heath care, tourism, pharma, real estate and, retail, etc. which have a direct impact on the opportunities available in these sectors. The rapid development of the banking and insurance sectors in the private sector, automobile, F.M.C.G., telecommunication, fashion and accessories, and unprecedented growth in e-commerce in last one-two years have opened up new windows for the youth for employment. In infrastructure sector, new possibilities have opened up in construction, roads, electricity, water, defense, telecom, and airlines etc. In traditional agricultural sector also, besides the cultivation of cereals, new areas like growing fruits, flowers, vegetables, and animal husbandry have developed fast. These sectors have not only created new jobs, but have created interest in setting up private enterprises among people. Moreover, the government's new policies and encouragement have resulted in an environment where today's young generation is more interested in becoming an entrepreneur. Setting up private enterprises is now easier and as a result more and more youth are getting attracted in setting up such ventures. Job opportunities in foreign countries have also risen resulting in more youth being attracted towards grabbing these opportunities.

When so much of opportunities of variety are available in India and abroad, it is a huge responsibility for the today's youth to explore and decide a right career prospect of one's own choice as it has far-reaching consequences for the whole life of that young man.

Therefore, it is essential that today's youth determine his future in a very careful manner after taking into account all possibilities and choose a right career for himself. Nowadays, right time to choose career is after Class X itself, when a young man choose his career as per his skills, capabilities and interest. Every young man should be quite prudent in the selection process and knowing the limited understanding and maturity level of a Class X student, it is essential that the youngster consults his parents, guardians, teachers and other well-wishers. Other than elders in family, it is advantageous to consult other youths who are three-four years senior in age and experience as their experience is contemporary and more relevant than others. In today's time, it is better to take experts' opinion who specialize in giving right career advice based upon a person or their qualities. For this purpose, many written, verbal, and psychological tests are also developed, whose test results conclusively indicate which career option would be more appropriate for a child or youth, for instance, medical, engineering, management, administrative, advocacy, etc. Therefore, it is necessary for a young man that he goes through these processes and reach a definitive opinion. Two years period after Class X is very precious and critical till a student do not take his Class XII exams. In fact, at the time of Class X examination, a student has to also decide upon which stream he wants to take, i.e. Science, Arts or Commerce, and as I said earlier, each student has to take up this call based upon his interest, skill, and capabilities.

Studies up to Class X, results and student's interest towards a stream play important role in the choice of stream. A Science stream student primarily aims for engineering, medical or higher education in science stream itself, i.e. graduation, post-graduation, Ph.D. etc. Similarly for Arts stream students, opportunities are open for higher studies and competing in different competitive exams. Arts stream youths often aim for employment in administrative posts, banking, management, and teaching. Commerce stream students opt for careers in C.A., C.S., cost accountancy, management, etc. in addition to higher studies. All these choice and information must be minutely given to the children and youths so that they get a proper base for taking a wise decision. It will be unfair to impose any decision upon them and it is often seen that imposed decision is harmful in long run. Science stream students in their plus two, i.e. XI and XII classes either choose Physics, Chemistry, Mathematics or Biology. Most children opting for mathematics go for engineering as career option and students opting for biology choose to pursue a career in medical science. For both categories, it is very important to have proper studies in plus two and also to participate in competitive exams that are held after plus two board examinations. On one side, there is a tough competition to score well in plus two board examination, on the other side, there is even much harder competition to clear I.I.T. and P.M.T. competitive exams as higher ranks in these exams are prerequisite for admission in any good institution. To do well in plus two examinations, it is absolutely necessary to be regular in school, in-depth studies of NCERT books and other popular additional books, and solving the previous year question banks. It is necessary to take guidance from teachers. Nowadays, it is generally seen in each city and locality that children opt for coaching and often students acknowledge about the benefits of the same. Students join reputed national level coaching institutions like FITJEE, Vidya Mandir, Pace, Bansal, Chaitnaya etc. for preparing for entrance exams of I.I.T. or other engineering colleges and they get benefit in competitive exams. For medical, institutions like Aakash are considered more successful. It is essential for students to deliberate considerably before opting for science stream and then be ready to work hard for two years once they have opted for this stream. Continuous hard work and consistent learning only bring them expected results. Here, it is noteworthy that all competitive exams take place in April or after that and forms for the same are filled between November to January. Admission process completes in June-July through counselling after declaration of results.

Students of Commerce stream also aim to score good marks in board examinations after completing plus two studies as very high percentage of marks is required for admission in under-graduation courses in Delhi University or other universities. Commerce graduates aim for C.A. or C.S. degrees for which they need to clear different examinations in addition to articleship which is not easy. Other students opt for management courses or post-graduation after their graduation.

Students of arts streams also need to put hard work in plus two studies as for admission in graduation require quite a high percentage is required. Later in different competitive exams also questions of plus two levels are included. There are many subject options available for students opting for graduation from arts or science stream like Economics, Sociology, Philosophy, Political Science, History, English literature, Hindi literature, Sanskrit, etc. Science stream students can also study Physics, Chemistry, Mathematics, Statistics, Operations Research, Zoology, Geology, and Life Sciences, etc. Admission process in each university is different, though primarily it is based upon marks percentage in most of the places. In many universities, e.g. in Delhi University, written exams or interviews are conducted separately for some colleges or in some subjects. It is beneficial to do graduation from prestigious universities like Delhi University and nowadays there are chances of campus placement at the end of third and final year. Many companies from India and abroad give placements to students on very good salary. And this change has been observed mainly in last few years. Earlier, options were limited and full of struggle, for example, for an economics graduate. A hardworking economics graduate used to first try for civil services and if he cleared the exam, it was satisfying or else, he used to search for other options. The other options included I.E.S. Examination, banking, R.B.I., SAIL, SIDBI examinations or else he used to try for lectureship. Today, though all these options still exist, yet due to campus placement, many new options have opened up in national/international companies. If one looks beyond economics, then considerable options are there in subjects like history, political science and social sciences etc. Another option available is law after graduation, though now five years integrated course in law is more popular.

Here it is important to describe that in recent decades spread of professional courses also grew in addition to general graduation courses and there is higher demand for professional graduates. Many new courses like BBA, BCA, Fashion Designing, Hotel Management, Para-Medicals and many other vocation courses have also become popular and students are preferring them over general graduation courses.

It can therefore be concluded that in today's and future socio-economic circumstances, there is no dearth of opportunities for the youth rather these opportunities will grow with time. There will be more opportunities in new sectors and new skill for the youth shall be in demand. More options will be available abroad. It is therefore necessary that every youth works hard in a targeted direction with full determination. He will definitely be successful. Yes, it is important that he keeps taking complete and right information while deciding his path, learning and putting hard work.

□

3

MBA, How is this Destination

When Keshav reached his neighbor Shivam Bhaiya's house, there was festival-like celebration at the house. Guests were congratulating Shivam and praising about his success to his parents. Sweets were being distributed to everyone. Shivam, who was studying in country's renowned management college, got campus placement, i.e. he got job from the college itself and he had to join the job immediately after completing his study in next few months. A big multi-national company in India had selected Shivam on a very good salary. Shivam's parents were very delighted and feeling proud and Shivam also seemed very happy. He was now dreaming to be successful like select few corporate leaders who were world renowned professionals. Keshav was happy for the success of Shivam Bhaiya and was very eager to know about his future and especially about management education and its related career. Shivam Bhaiya was not just a friend but an ideal for him. His success had raised Keshav's curiosity and eagerness and he wanted to know more and more about management education and its related career opportunities.

Further discussion is in context of lacs of youth like Keshav who are curious and eager to know about management education and career. In today's date and in future to come, there is a great scope for management-related career which is a good sign for youth and they can certainly choose management as their career. Rising global economy, increasing markets and trade, growing demands among people and society, all have positive impact on corporate world and companies, businesses, trade are all growing with time and hence there is better demand for managers for handling their operations.

There is a fast growing demand for managers and related jobs with management not only in private sector but in government and public sector as well. In simple terms, for selling, marketing or advertising, for keeping accounts or for financial management, to employ people or to manage human resources, everywhere managers are needed and for that skilled and experienced people are required. Be it company, government, NGO, public sector or private sector, everyone needs good skilled managers for their different tasks.

Seeing the growing demand for skilled and experienced managers, management as a career has got popularized in our country and today's youth irrespective of engineering, science, arts or commerce background is adopting management as a career. There are many institutions in the country for pursuing management career. Basically, there are four types of institutions. In first category, there are topmost institutions IIMs whose number stands 20 today. Among them oldest and most prestigious are Ahmedabad, Bangalore, Kolkata and Lucknow. After IIMs, there are AICTE-approved autonomous institutions which are about 300 in number and they all run Post Graduate Diploma in Management programs. Some selected and leading institutions are given in Appendix 1.

Their list can be seen in some leading magazines that publish B-schools rankings like *Business India, Business World,* and *Competition Success Review,* etc. or can also be seen on management education-related websites. Apart from a list of handful institutions given in the appendix, management institutions are spread in almost every state in the country. It is another matter that their quality and credibility differ.

Institutions which are related to one or the other university are kept in third category and they provide MBA degree. Included in this category are FMS of Delhi University or management departments of IITs Besides private universities like ICFAI, Narsee Monjee Mumbai may also be included in this category. Fourth category consists of world-renowned institutions like ISB Hyderabad which are highly regarded in the corporate world, though they are neither affiliated to any university nor they are recognized by AICTE.

In addition to these four categories of P.G. institutions, there are plenty of institutions providing under-graduate level education which provide BBA degree. Admission is done after 12th class in these institutions and students further study for MBA or PGDM after getting BBA degree from these institutions.

Among these four categories of post-graduate courses, a course that is related to a university and provide MBA degree is a degree course. Other institutions including IIMs, those offer post-graduate diploma in management provide diploma after completion of the course.

From a practical perspective, as far as employment is concerned, there is no difference in both degree and diploma, rather in actual practice it is true that there are better job opportunities available in IIMs and other diploma offering management institutions. Of course, if someone wants to go for further higher studies, i.e. Ph.D., then simple diploma is not eligible as only MBA degree holders are eligible there. However, this limitation is not a hurdle for diploma holders provided diploma of an institution has been provided MBA equivalence by Association of Indian Universities (AIU).

Anyone with an AIU approved diploma can do Ph.D. as that diploma is equivalent to MBA degree. For that purpose, an institution has to apply to AIU for according equivalence to MBA degree status to its diploma.

As previously mentioned, it is necessary to have some university affiliation for the institutions offering MBA programs. This university can either be government or private. Post Graduate Diploma in Management (PGDM) course is offered by IIMs and other institutions. All courses of IIMs are independently recognized but other institutions have to take AICTE approval each year for their PGDM courses.

It is noteworthy here that employment opportunities are very rare for unapproved courses except for institutions like ISB Hyderabad which have their own standing and reputation in the industry. Hence, it is essential for students and parents that they carefully check AICTE approval for any course before taking admission. This information is available on institution's website or can also be inquired from AICTE. If required, one can ask for AICTE recognition letter from the institute. Here, it is important to know that this recognition is not to the institute but to the course run by the institution. Many a times, many institutions run multiple management courses e.g. PGDM, PGDM (Finance), PGDM (Marketing), PGDM (Retail), PGDM (Services Marketing) etc. for which there is separate enrollment. An institution needs to take separate approval for all such courses. Often, it has been seen that among many courses run by an institution, only one or two are AICTE approved and all other courses are run without approval. Students must not take admission in non-approved courses. Hence, it is necessary that before taking admission in any institution, first of all one must inquire status of approval of its management course. Then if one wants to opt for Ph.D. in future, then it is necessary to inquire A.I.U.'s MBA equivalence status for that PGDM course. A.I.U. recognition makes that diploma equivalent to MBA.

Apart from this, if one wants to judge an institution and its program quality and credibility then it is necessary to pay attention to two other recognitions. A course accredited by National Board of Accreditation (NBA) is considered superior in quality than others. Similarly, quality of an institution or its course can also be checked/measured by NAAC recognition and even above them if some institution or its courses are recognized by international agencies like AMBA, SAQS then it's superiority is better established. There are other parameters also to measure quality for a better institution which will be discussed separately under Admission topic.

□

4

Enrollment in MBA and Preparation

MBA or PGDM, both are post-graduation courses, in which enrollment is done after receiving graduation degree. These courses are for two years duration and generally these courses begin between mid-June to mid-July. Some universities start MBA course from August or September. The enrollment process, however, begins almost one year before from September month itself. For example, for 2018 session, enrollment process would start in September 2017 itself. Interested students also need to know that these courses are full-time course and after enrolling in this course, no other full time course can be under taken parallel to it. As mentioned earlier, this course begins from June/July and ends in April/May of second year and one has to join a company immediately after completion in case of campus placement. During this period, one has to undergo full course either in six trimesters (four months) or four semesters (six months) mode. Exams take place after each trimester or semester and final result is based upon total marks obtained in all the exams. At the end of first year, when three trimesters or two semesters are completed, students have to undergo six-eight weeks of summer internship, where student has to work in association with a company and its evaluation is also included in final result. Hence, students have to be fully alert towards summer internship and have to work systematically during their internship. In fact, students have no scope for any long vacations during these two years and they have to devote full two years to complete this course.

Minimum education qualification for both MBA and PGDM is graduation and a student has to score minimum 50 per cent marks in graduation. There is some relaxation for SC/ST or OBC category students and students with even lesser than 50 percent marks are considered eligible. It is necessary to qualify in 10th and 12th exams which is but natural, though there is no minimum score prescribed for these two exams. Students appearing in final year examination in current session may also apply for enrollment and can also be provisionally admitted in case of selection but they have to submit their graduation result by September of first session or else they stand disqualified.

Students meeting the above criteria may apply in different institutions. They have to apply separately in each institution. Application process is primarily online in most of the institutions. Course-related brochure can also be downloaded online and application fee can also be paid online. Application process starts in September but its commencement and end dates have to be checked at an institution's website.

Students who meet the minimum norms have to clear qualifying examination also in addition to applying in different institutions and institutions offer admissions based upon merit list. Students have to appear in multi-level examinations. First of all written examination is conducted and institutions invite students for next round based upon written exam score. Next round involves group discussion and personal interviews. Finally, admission is offered based upon cumulative score of written exam, group discussion and interview. One formula to prepare merit list among different formula & applied could be giving fifty per cent weightage to written exam, twenty per cent each to group discussion and interview and rest ten percent for the work experience (i.e. past job experience). This way students' percentage is calculated on a scale of 100 and merit list is prepared. It entirely depends upon the institutions which formula they opt for. Students are offered admission from the merit list based upon available seats in an institution.

Written exam for enrollment in MBA or PGDM is conducted at national level and different agencies conduct the same. First of all, written exam for enrollment is for IIMs which is conducted by one of the IIM itself and is called CAT (Common Admission Test). After passing CAT exam and based upon score obtained one can participate in IIM admission process. CAT exam is conducted once in a year mostly in November. Nowaday-exams take place online and its pattern is objective type. Duration of examination is three hours. In 200-300 marks question paper, there are three or four sections, whose details are given below.

Other than IIMs, many leading and other institutions make use of CAT exam score as the base for enrollment process. Apart from CAT, there are many other exams also like MAT, CMAT, and ATMA which are used by institutions for their enrollment process. All these exams are conducted by different agencies or institutions. MAT is conducted by AIMA (All India Management Association). Similarly, CMAT and XAT are conducted by AICTE and XLRI, respectively. All these tests are recognized by the national institutions. All institutions recognize the score of these examinations. It is up to students in which examinations they want to appear and based upon the score obtained they participate in institution's enrollment process. A student can appear in more than one examination and can make his enrollment base to an exam result where he has scored higher. All other institutions except IIM recognize these exams and include students in their enrollment process based upon score obtained in any of these exams. As far as examination pattern is concerned, almost all exams define their pattern and sequence in accordance with CAT pattern. The difference is observed in simplicity/difficulty level of questions but all exams are objective type and are conducted online only.

MAT examination is conducted four times during a session. A student can appear in any of the September, December, March, and May exam and can enroll himself based on the score obtained in any of the four. There is possibility of improving the score in next MAT exam if he is not able to score good marks in one particular MAT exam. CMAT and XAT are conducted once in a year like CAT. CAT exam, as said above, is conducted once and in the month of November. For instance, in one of the recent past years, it was conducted on 29th November and exams centres were kept in about 130 cities all over India. Approximately, 2,16,000 students had applied for the CAT exam and approximately 1,90,000 finally appeared for the examination. Among students giving CAT exams, most of them also appear in MAT and other examinations expecting better score in those exams. A large number of students appear only in MAT or CMAT exams. These students are not eligible for IIMs or in the institutions which accept only CAT score as the basis for their enrollment. These students can appear only those institutions which accept enrollment based upon MAT, CMAT, or XAT in addition to CAT.

As a next stage of enrollment, IIMs and other institutions make written exam CAT, MAT, CMAT, XAT score the base, as applicable, and declare a minimum cutoff, and call students scoring above that cutoff for next round of enrollment process. For example, each IIM declares minimum cutoff in CAT independently for their campus. This cutoff point is in percentile, which means, for example, 80 out of 100 students are below a student who has scored

80 percentile. Usually, IIMs minimum cutoff are above 95 percentile and only those students are invited for next round whose percentile is 95 or above. Cutoff percentile below 95 may go for some new IIMs like Ranchi, Trichi, Kashipur, Udaipur, Raipur, Rohtak. Moreover, many IIMs determine the sectional cutoff also and on that basis decide the enrollment process. Sectional cutoff for sections like Verbal ability or Quantitative analytics are declared and a student has to meet both overall percentile cutoff and sectional cutoff to get a call, i.e. to take part in next round of enrollment process. Similar criteria is followed by the institutions which consider CAT, MAT, CMAT, XAT score as the basis for enrollment.

Next round of enrollment process is group discussion round. In simple terms, group discussion can be understood from day to day example wherein daily life some people, some friends or classmates sit together to discuss any topic. Everybody put forward his views in this discussion and this way discussion becomes increasingly interesting. Such discussions can be seen from the drawing room to the tea or beetle shops. Same is the case with group discussion, where a group of students is formed with approximately 10 students and they have to discuss in ten to fifteen minutes on a given topic. Discussion topic is decided by institution representatives and they take care of time limit also. Five minutes time is given to students before starting formal discussion to think on and for preparing the topic. Most of the time, the topic is related to contemporary economic, social, political and other intellectual issues. Topic is chosen in such a way that opinion can be formed both in favour and against the topic and some members speak for the motion and others speak against the motion. Examiners are present during the discussion, who assess the group members and give marks based on assessment.

There are several aspects to assess the group discussion,

such as:

- Personality of students.
- Student's normal behavior in group with peers and behavior during discussions.
- Student's communication ability (ability to speak) and skills, in which along with English-speaking, correct pronunciation, use of right words, right rhythm are measured.
- Cooperation or non-cooperation of a student with other members in the group.
- Grip of the student on the subject and based upon subject knowledge and rhetoric, ability to give proper direction to the discussion.
- Put forward his views in front of members and to build consensus on those views.
- From above points, leadership quality of a particular student is also measured.
- Student giving chances to other members also to speak that reflects his team spirit.

Mainly experts monitor these aspects only and give marks according to their assessment. Many times it is seen that all members of the group become agitated during the discussion and debate become unplanned. Many institutions have adopted separate methods to overcome this problem, such as giving each student two-three minutes time to put forward his views on given subject instead of group discussion. Some institutions use both. Some other institutions include case analysis. In case analysis, there is description of an event or a situation and student has to answer few questions after reading the description. These questions are related to the given incident or event. Student is required to answer questions in writing. With this examiner would like to know about student's knowledge of the English language and his command over language. They also want to know student's ability to assess and analyze a given situation. Thirdly, they assess how the student forms his opinion after analyzing the situation. All these angles, are hidden in the asked questions.

After group discussions, or case analysis, next round is of personal interview. In interview panel, there are three or four experts. This panel is constituted of experienced faculty of the institute and industry experienced professionals. Many a times, institutes prefer to keep experts also in the panel. Though there is no fix time frame for an interview, yet generally it is of 15-20 minutes duration, in which panel experts ask questions on every aspect from the student. Family, personal and academic background details are asked minutely and related questions are asked. Through interview, on one hand, experts try to understand the person, on other hand they also judge how transparent and honest is a student, as often students overstat many things which are different from reality thinking that such things will influence the panel. Apart from this, student skills are evaluated based upon subject knowledge, general knowledge, comments and views on contemporary topics and system as related questions are asked. By giving them some practical situation, it is tried to understand how and what they will decide in a given situation. Their personality type is also explored by giving some special circumstances and as a final question it is explored if the student will be able to adapt himself according to industry conditions, or if he will be able to take right decision and adopt best working style in industrial environment or not. Interviewers try to find out answers of all these questions. A student who is found to meet all these criteria, his interview marks are above normal otherwise he is given normal or below normal marks.

After completing all three stages of enrollment, final merit list of any institution is prepared and according to that list, successful students are given offer letter or invited for enrollment. Merit list is also brought out in different stages. Generally, merit list up to three stages are published. If a student's name doesn't appear in first list then he should wait till second or third list. If student's name is appearing even in waiting list, then it is probable that his name will come in subsequent second or third list.

Once the name is appearing in a list, then he can reserve his seat by depositing first installment of the fee for the course and it is mandatory. As far as group discussion or personal interview are concerned, these are organized in different cities of the country and students have facility to attend the same in their nearest city but for fees or enrollment process they have to contact the institution directly if not personally then through email, phone or correspondence. Fees can also be deposited through draft or net banking. In case of withdrawal (for getting admission in better institution or for any other reason) before commencement of the course only one thousand rupees is deducted as institution is obliged to return the balance amount. It is in AICTE rules and if an institution puts obstruction in releasing the rest amount, then complaint of the institution has to be lodged to AICTE and its hearing is compulsory. After commencement of the course, institution can deduct proportionate amount in case of withdrawal of nomination. Details of the same are available on AICTE website.

Course fees vary depending on the institution, which may range starting from 3-4 lacs to 15 lacs and even upwards for two years. Fee consists of tuition fees, development fee, study material fee, examination fee, library fee, IT fee, etc. In addition, hostel fee and mess fee are also there. In leading institutions including IIMs this course is entirely residential, i.e. no student can live outside campus. He cannot study staying at his home or with relatives. In this case, hostel and mess fees are mandatory. Where this is not mandatory, students who live outside do not have to pay this fee. Many institutions include foreign trip, laptop, iPad, dress, etc. in their course, cost of all this is essentially included in the total fee. Each institution's website or brochure mentions total fee, its breakup and due dates of installments. Students must see and understand the same. It is important to note that based on these fee details and on enrollment/admission documents, banks provide education loan and to complete the formalities, these two documents are a must. For any recognized course, loan can be availed from any government or private sector banks of one's own city, which students can repay in monthly installments after placement or after course completion.

Many institutions offer scholarships also to promote merit, which give some percentage of relief in the total fee. Most scholarship schemes are based on graduation marks percentage, and score in CAT, MAT, CMAT, etc. which benefit the meritorious student in the first year. To continue its benefit in second year also, a student has to score certain minimum percentage of marks in first year exams.

We saw above and understood that one has to appear in primarily three types of exams for enrollment. First written examination which are CAT, MAT, CMAT, XAT like examinations, second examination is in the form of group discussion and third exam is personal interview or interaction. Here we should devote some time on matters related to preparation for these examinations.

First we will understand about written examinations like CAT, MAT. Generally, these tests are of two to three hours duration and of 200 and 300 marks. These tests have mainly three sections, i.e. quantitative ability, verbal and reading comprehension and data interpretation and logical reasoning. Syllabus for these sections is given in the following table, which is only indicative and not exhaustive.

Quantitative Ability	**Verbal Ability**	**Data Interpretation**	**Logical Reasoning**
Algebra	Sentence Correction	Pie Chart	Data Arrangement
Geometry	Para Jumble	Bar Graph	Seating Arrangement
Number System	Para Completion	Line Graph	Blood Relation
Mathematics	Fact Inference	Tables	Family Tree
Higher Maths	Judgment	Caselet	Venn Diagram
Mensuration	Word Usages	Data Sufficiency	Matching
			Puzzles
Trigonometry	Vocabulary	Syllogism	Preposition
Sub Topics	Fill in the blank		Assumption
• H.C.F.	Grammar		Statements
• L.C.M.			Binary Logic
• A.P.			Clock
• G.P.			Calendar
• G.M.			Information
• H.M			
• Median			
• Mode			
• Ratio and Proportion			
• Percentage			
• Average			
• Partnership			
• Time, speed, distance			
• Work and time			
• Profit and loss			
• Partnership			
• Pipe and System			
• Lines			
• Angle, Triangle, Cube, etc.			

Questions in the examination are based around these topics or sub-topics only, although it has also been observed that every year some newness is there in the questions and it actually depends on students' skills and preparation if those questions are solved or not. Students have to prepare on the basis of above syllabus only. For preparation it is necessary that student buy Guide related to CAT, MAT and make the same an integral part of their preparation. Guides from various prestigious publications are available in the market for CAT, MAT preparation. In addition, it is observed that every successful student is also attached with some coaching institute. In the country, many certified and well-known institutions provide coaching for CAT, MAT preparation. Among these institutions IMS, TIME, Career Launcher, etc. are more popular, where majority of students take coaching. Information of all these institutions can be taken from their websites. At present, these institutions have presence in all major cities of the country. These coaching institutes also provide reading material along with classroom coaching, which can be used for practice at home by the student. Further, these institutes make the students to solve question papers based on CAT/ MAT model on regular or equal intervals and exams are taken so that students get practice and they can also judge their progress.

Two types of students join management career. First category is of the students who appear in CAT/MAT exam immediately after graduation, engineering or any other graduation degree in the same year and take admission in the same year. In second category come those students who participate in management education enrollment process after working two to three years on completion of engineering or other graduation courses. In both cases, almost a year preparation is needed which include self-study, coaching, etc. It is also essential that student has taken his studies seriously right from school education till graduation, especially Mathematics and English which have greater weightage in the written examination. Along with students, it is equally necessary for the parents who wish to send their children in management discipline that they pay special attention on their wards' education from school level itself. They need to ensure that children foundation is strong in Math, English and/or other subjects.

The second round examination, as mentioned above, is the group discussion. For group discussion, it is necessary to have good command over English, can speak good English, i.e. style, grammar and vocabulary all are in order. For this, it is essential to pay attention from school level itself. Along with written English, equal attention needs to be paid on speaking and pronunciation. Conversing in English with friends, classmates and peers at home prove beneficial. Student must develop habit of listening to English news, talks, read English newspapers and magazines, all these will benefit him in group discussion.

Along with English skills it is also necessary for success in group discussion that student has knowledge of Current Affairs, i.e. contemporary topics, circumstances, events, etc. and is fully aware of their nuances. Regular habit of reading newspaper and magazines and studying different subjects right from school days onwards is very useful and enable students such that they speaking meaningful on topics of group discussion and may give their opinion. During group discussions, examiner pays most attention on student opinion formation along with communication skills. Therefore, it is necessary that student study more and more and keep a close eye on contemporary topics. Coaching institutes generally prepare for group discussion. For example, in recently concluded sessions few topics picked up were:

- Paris COP 21: Epic Fail or Best chance to save the planet?
- Returning Sahitya Academy Awards, Is it a right kind of Protest?
- Economic status – a reasonable criteria for reservations.
- Poverty causes corruption.
- Should India have a one-child policy?
- Made in India or Make in India.
- GST is it a boon or a bane for economy? Is parliamentary democracy good for India?

These few examples are not enough to show how many and how different topics can be! Yet these at least indicate how intensively students have to prepare.

In third phase, students have to face personal interview or interaction. Students must prepare substantially for interview, be it subjects' knowledge, general knowledge or current affairs. It is also important not to panic during interview, do not feel stressed and face panel normally. It is necessary to keep in mind while responding to the panel, to answer honestly and to the extent you know and what is right. It is for sure that in case of lying or exaggerating the facts, panel will come to know and it will have adverse effect. Students must understand that panel members are experienced people and can differentiate between truth and lies easily. Students must take advice from experienced counsellors of coaching institutions for facing personal interview. They should also take advantage of their seniors' experiences. Proper guidance may also be available from elders in family and family members working in the corporate world. Personal interview-related videos are available on Internet and one can take their benefit. Along with all these, mock interviews in coaching institutions or at other places are also very useful and students must repeatedly take them for practice. Students must make videos of such mock interviews and try to identify their weaknesses from them. On eve of personal interview or on interview day, it is essential to keep cool, open mind and not to take any kind of stress. Keeping in mind all these nuances will ensure a good interview.

□

5

Selection of MBA Institutions

After understanding the whole process of enrollment and how to prepare for the same, it is also important to know how to choose the institution. What are those factors that need to be kept in mind while selecting the institution? Question of institute's selection raises in two stages. First, while applying for enrollment, and second when student is selected at more than one institution in the enrollment process and gets multiple call letters.

From among the key considerations while applying, it is necessary to pay attention on following points:

1. Assess confidence of your ability and decide if CAT exam is to be given or not. And if it is to be given then to self-introspect if preparations are of IIM level or not, i.e. if 95 or above percentile can be obtained or not. Most students willing to pursue a brighter career in management decide in "Yes" to this question and sit in CAT examination for enrollment in IIMs without any doubt. The number of such students in 2015 was more than two lacs. Hence, if self-assessment answer is in "Yes", then it is mandatory to apply for CAT exam.
2. For enrollment in IIMs, one needs to apply for CAT examination only. Separate application in different IIMs is not needed. Based upon CAT result,

different IIMs decide their cutoff percentile and call the students for next round of group discussion or personal interview.

3. In case of selection in more than one IIM, students have to choose one. Usually, in order of preference Ahmedabad stands first, Bangalore second, Calcutta third, Lucknow fourth followed by Indore and rest of the IIMs. Students choose one based upon this parameter only. Rather than taking admissions in new IIMs, many students prefer other leading institutions in the country such as MDI, S.P. Jain, IMT, FMS, XLRI, IMI and others outside the IIM umbrella.
4. The first goal of students appearing in CAT exam is IIM but if not selected there, then no one wants to take risk or do not want to waste a year, so they apply in many leading institutions mentioned above. These leading institutions primarily enroll students based upon CAT score only, except XLRI which conducts its own independent examination XAT. Many other institutions also give recognition to XAT in addition to CAT.

   Such students need to apply separately in these institutions. All of them are recognized by AICTE or institutions like FMS (Delhi University) which are affiliated with some recognized university.
5. Many students looking for a career in management are not sure even after appearing in CAT exam if they will get good result, they don't take risk and appear in MAT or CMAT exam and apply for the same. Majority of the management institutions in the country enroll primarily based on MAT or CMAT score only apart from CAT. For such institutions, students have to apply separately in each institution where they want to enroll.

At the time of applying to these institutions, it is necessary to ensure that courses of these institutions are recognized by AICTE. At the time of application, location of the institute, its market reputation, fees conformity with the budget, all these factors need to be taken into consideration.

6. In case of selection in more than one institution, for selecting any one institution, few basic points must be kept in mind and a decision can be taken making those points as the basis of selection.
   A. In addition to, being recognized by AICTE, if the institution courses are certified by institutions like AIU, NBA or NAAC or not. Significance and quality of course increases if the course is certified by all three or at least one or two of these bodies. AIU recognition gives PGDM diploma a status equivalent to the MBA degree.
   B. Some leading institutions have got international accreditation like MDI, IMI, S.P. Jain. Recognition of such institutions is definitely better than others.
   C. To assess the quality of management institutes in the country and grading them, there are many popular rankings which rank 100-200 management institutions in the country every year. More prevalent among them are CSR-GHRDC, Business World, Business Today, Business India, Career 360, MBA Universe, NHRD, etc. Students and parents can make comparison or draw conclusion based upon these rankings. All these ranking agencies collect data from institutions and inspect those institutions before publishing final rankings. Base of these rankings are institute's placement records, industry relationships, quality of faculty, research, MDP, library facilities, IT-related services and

institution's infrastructure. It is necessary for students and parents that they seriously study these points and do a comparative study to reach at a conclusion. It is also necessary to discuss with ex-students (from alumni), current students, and faculty of the institute to learn more about the institute. This would require a personal visit to the institute and to understand the information given on the institution's website. Opinion of alumni, students and experts can also be taken from some websites like shiksha.com, pagalguy.com, on which people very actively discuss the virtues or shortcomings of institutions.

D. Placement – In placement information, it is necessary to know what percentage of the total students get campus placement. If it is 90 percent or more, it should be considered good. Simultaneously, it is also important to know the average and maximum package and which all and what type of companies come for placement.

E. Relation with Industry – How much engaged is the institution with the industry and what arrangements have been made by the institution for industry connect. Where these relations are strong and proper arrangements are in place, there students get a chance to associate with industry, and to learn industry functioning by working there. This would benefit not just the placement but student get benefits in further career also. With good arrangements, students get better summer internships and also get opportunity to meet industry experts and learn from them.

F. Faculty – It is necessary to have faculty in the institution but even more important is quality of the faculty. In management discipline, faculty is required to provide not only subject knowledge but equally important is to give practical aspects of the same in a manner which can be utilized in industrial or in actual conditions. It is necessary to give training to the students so that they can find out the solution meticulously in most serious and unexpected circumstances. For that it is necessary that faculty of the institute is well qualified, experienced and have industry experience and if not have the industry experience still they have connect and attraction towards the industry, so that they have knowledge about developments in the industry which they can pass on to the students. Similarly, it is also essential to know faculty experience, their tenure in teaching, Ph.D. status, exposure about India and other countries, their research and relationship with companies. Faculty is the foundation of an institution which has to be strong. Strong faculty base proves a better institution.

G. Research – Another important aspect related to facuity is research, which establishes strong hold of faculty on their subjects, makes them aware of contemporary development in the subject and new discoveries. Students get the benefit of the same in the class and in their studies. Faculty is able to get updated information of current trends in industry across the globe through research. Faculty research-related information can be obtained from the institute's website or library. Sound research by faculty gives much credibility to the institution and connect them to government, society and industry which in turn benefit the students and they also get new opportunities.

H. Library and IT-related Benefits – It is also necessary to know about books, journals, magazines, newspapers, videos, audios, etc. available in the library Institutions where all these facilities are available, they are in students' interest. Similarly, IT facilities like Wi-Fi, LMS, computer, printer, scanner, video conferencing, seminar facility are essential for students in current time and must be considered while choosing an institution.

I. Infrastructure – Generally, all institutions pay attention towards maintenance of the entire campus, classrooms, auditorium, library, IT lab, hostels, mess, faculty, and all other facilities, still, these also need to be looked into while choosing the campus. Also, one should convince himself about maintenance of the campus, security arrangements and student's care of an institution. If institutions are evaluated in terms of these points, then it is easier to reach a fair conclusion and decision won't be wrong. It has to be understood that parents or students should not enroll themselves blindly in any institutions without proper inquiry. There are several institutions which make great promises and send letter of nomination to students and students from remote and interior countryside enroll themselves without proper inquiry. Later they have to regret as reality of these institutions is different from what they were promised. Similarly, there are many consultants in the market who mislead the students for their interests. It is strongly advised to avoid them.

□

6

Two Challenging Years of MBA

Course starts with orientation/induction program in each institution with time duration ranging from a week to fifteen days. Purpose of the orientation or induction program is to make aware the student about institute's environment, its activities, rules and regulations related to course curriculum. Since new batch of students come from different corners of the country and differ significantly in their background, living style, personality and in communication style, therefore attempts are made to introduce them to institute's culture and develop harmony amongst all during the induction program. In induction program, many activities are conducted to achieve this objective. Students should very actively participate in these activities. Attendance is made mandatory for the whole orientation/induction program by the institute and students and parents are informed well in advance for the same so that they can plan journey and ensure presence. It is a big opportunity for students where they can showcase their talent and personality and establish their reputation in the whole batch. Students get ample opportunities to show their talent in competition like Talent-Hunt and institutes also give them many opportunities in future in debate, plays, music, dance, painting, etc. after learning about their unique talent.

In addition to orientation/induction program, many institutions also organize foundation course ranging from ten to fifteen days. In foundation course, primarily subjects like accounting, finance, statistics, quantitative techniques, economics and information technology, etc. are taught so that students coming from different streams may have a basic knowledge of these subjects and it becomes easier to explain these subjects in regular course. It is very useful opportunity for students which they must take advantage of. In today's time, many institutions even go beyond this and help students in preparing for the course much in advance. After paying enrollment fee, institutions offer online studies facility so that students study and learn many subjects before joining the institution. Institutions also connect a faculty with each student with whom student can contact over phone or through email. Arrangements are made to connect with subject faculty so that students can get help while learning online if needed. Students must take benefit of all these facilities.

Regular classes start after orientation/induction program. As mentioned earlier, the whole course is divided in six trimesters or four semesters. In addition, there is summer internship of six to eight weeks. According to AICTE rules, minimum 1050 hours studies is mandatory in full course and also six weeks summer internship. It is flexibility of the institutions how they design the whole course syllabus. MBA courses under universities purview follow the syllabus fixed by university, though each course's syllabus may differ. A broad structure of the syllabus is given below :

Term I	Term II	Term III
Accounting for Decision Making	Business Communication II	Business Communication III
		Entrepreneurship
Business Communication I	Financial Management I	Financial Management II

		Human Resource Management
Information Technology for Management	Macro Economics & Business Environment	IT for Effective Decision Making
Managerial Economics	Management Accounting & Control	Operations Management
Marketing Management I	Marketing Management II	Research Methods in Management
Organizational Behavior I	Organizational Behavior II	
Quantitative Analysis for Management I	Quantitative Analysis for Management II	
Term IV	**Term V**	**Term VI**
Legal Aspects of Management	Strategic Management II	Elective (2)
Strategic Management I		
Electives (5)	Electives (5)	

In above given syllabus, there are 23 core subjects and 12 electives. It is possible that they differ according to institution and according to the course. Core subjects have to be necessarily studied by all students. Electives are the subjects those are chosen by a student as per his specialization and for a specialization it is necessary to take 5-7 electives. For selecting 5-7 electives, a student has option of minimum 10 to 12 subjects from which they can choose necessary electives of their choice. Normally, areas of specialization are marketing, finance, HR, IT Operations and International Business, etc. Meaning of specialization is that a student of that specialization wants to build a career in that area only and after acquiring expertise in that area, they start their job also in that area. For example, student of marketing specialization wants to build a career in marketing only and they study 5-7 electives in marketing to get specialized knowledge. They also try to get marketing job as per their interest during placement process and begin their career in the same area. Institutions offer two types of specializations minor-major specialization and dual. In case of minor-major specialization, more electives are to be studied for major specialization and lesser for minor and during placement students' first interest or preference is to get job in major area only. In dual specialization, both specializations have equal weightage and the student can choose any of the two area as his preference.

It is essential for students that they understand well their interest and assess fully which career they want to pursue or which career will give them satisfaction. For this purpose, along with self-assessment, elders, seniors and faculty opinions also matter a lot. Along with this current and next five year economic scenario, industry trends, employment demand in industry, all these issues must be specially studied so that one can reach to a right conclusion. Generally, in third trimester, industry experts guide the students and they explain current and contemporary context of industry in detail to students. Students must take its benefit. Besides, faculty also based upon their experience guide the students about opportunities available in their respective areas like marketing, finance, HR, etc. Once students determine their specialization, then they must study all subjects of that specialization minutely and must also be aware of development of the industry in that area. They must develop contacts with industry experts of that area and should take their guidance. Not only it enhances knowledge but also helps in establishing oneself in the industry.

All subjects, core or elective, are of 30 hours duration in trimester system. A textbook is given in each subject which student should study thoroughly. Along with this many other books and articles are also suggested for references which students should refer. Faculty take class lectures based upon these materials only and they expect that students should learn them thoroughly after the class. Each faculty tries to give practical knowledge of each concept to students and explain them how these concepts are or can be useful in real life and in industry. For example, if sales management is being taught then qualities of a salesman should also be practically demonstrated, even more essential is to demonstrate through a video real life scenario where a salesman is making sale using his qualities. In today's time, along with studying books, video is very effective medium. Other than video, 'cases' are also used for practical knowledge. In a case, concepts of a subject are explained by describing real scenario of industry. After describing real situation, problem is put before students and it is expected that they find solution of those problems using concepts learnt about that subject. This way, students' practical aspects are made stronger using cases for all subjects and they also develop decision-making skills by practicing these cases again and again. In other type of courses, different aspects of Indian and foreign companies are described, so that students learn about those companies working style, decisions taken by them during favorable and unfavorable conditions/situations. This is highly beneficial in developing students' practical knowledge and decision-making skills.

From 30 hours study in each subject, about 20 percent i.e. six hours are fixed for guest faculty. These guest faculty are industry experts who have strong hold on those subjects and they can put forward practical aspects used in industry among students. Students must be present in these guest lectures and along with gaining knowledge, they should develop contacts with guest faculty. They get multiple benefits through these contacts.

To connect with industry and learn their reality, 'live project' is very powerful medium. Students must take advantage of live projects related to each subject. Under live projects, a company wants solution of problem of any of their department or wants to get survey done either independently by the student or under guidance of faculty. For example, if a company wants to launch sports-shoes new model for the youth in the markets near Delhi University like Kamala Nagar, Shakti Nagar, Camp, etc. then company would like to have a market survey done so as to know the interest and demand of students residing there or to know about products offered by competition. Through such surveys, company can make its new launch more effective and successful. Companies take help of management institutions faculty and students in such surveys and ask them to conduct such surveys, draw conclusion and give suggestions. Such surveys are for two to three weeks duration and in this period students gain lot of knowledge about each aspect from markets to customers and they can connect subjects learnt in class to real scenario and understand the integrities of the subjects much better. During this exercise, students get benefit from guidance by company experts and faculty. Students' skills are enhanced by doing many such live projects in different subjects. Each student should look forward for more and more opportunities to do live projects during two year course. Institute's placement department, faculty, alumni, industry's guest, friends and acquaintance prove helpful in getting live projects.

Other than live projects, faculty also give 'desk project' in each area which is very useful. For example, in economics, review of India's international trade can be given in form of desk research wherein students have to analyze the India international trade during last one year and it is expected to learn, total trade trends, sector-wise trade, export-import details and country to which export is done and country from where import takes place. Students also have to learn impacts of these trends on foreign currency and on country's economy. For this study, students don't have to go to field or industry but they collect and analyze data using Internet, library, etc. Such projects are also very useful to students as they put more emphasis on practical knowledge other than bookish knowledge and students learn about economy, different sectors, industry and company through these projects and develop interest towards research. Such interest and acquired knowledge is very useful in future career also.

Group projects is integral part of each subject. It covers all aspects of a subject and it is expected from students that they should provide solution or answer to the problem, question or situation given in the group projects keeping in mind each aspect learnt in the subject. Students should do these projects with full dedication and prepare project reports sitting together and after proper discussion. A written project report needs to be submitted and then a power point presentation is to be made in front of whole class. Faculty or other students ask questions during presentation. It is very good and enlightening opportunity to know and understand minute details of project. Other than facts, presentation style, skills to answer questions, confidence are also evaluated in presentation and students must focus on these aspects. During full course, students must keep in mind following points:

A) Be regular in the class and miss minimum classes.
B) Make notes of topic covered in class and have their detailed study through text or reference books.
C) Give proper importance to class notes and faculty power point slides as they prove useful for examination to placement.
D) Understand all concepts or each subject thoroughly and keep in mind their practical use and practical examples. Pay attention to the examples given in the book and try to learn something from them.
E) Read all small-big cases related to each concept and

try to learn from them. Other than books, *Harvard Business Review* & Ivey cases are also available which students must learn.

F) See the videos available in library or on Internet related to the subject and note down the basic points. Speeches and related videos of leaders from different areas of India and abroad must be seen. One can learn a lot from details of their life, experience and their working style. Watching videos or reading books related to company, economy of India-abroad or social system are also beneficial:

G) Regularly read the daily newspaper to learn current affairs and for general knowledge. Read at least one general newspaper like *The Times of India, Hindustan Times, The Hindu,* etc. along with one business newspaper such as *The Economic Times, Business Standard,* and *Mint,* etc. Try to read English newspapers only so as to get good grip over English language.

In addition to the newspapers, magazines like *Business Today, Business World,* etc. should also be read. Nowadays, all these newspapers and magazines are available on-line also so reading them become easier. Besides, there are many useful sites on the net from which every type of information can be extracted. Now many mobile apps are available on smart phones also from which students get 24 x 7 hours facilities.

H) Along with self-study, it is very important that studies, discussions, subjects or cases are discussed in groups. Studies or discussions done in groups are very beneficial and students learn a lot from each other. Each student has his own thinking, wisdom which they share with each other resulting in higher understanding to all.

I) Stay in regular touch with faculty and understand every aspect of their subjects from them and request for tutorial classes whenever needed.

J) Many students do not just confine to own institution friends, but they remain in contact with students of other good institutions. They share subjects, cases, video, etc. with each other and that way teaching-learning boundaries become wider. Such a network among students is quite beneficial during placement and in career therefore students should pay special attention to this.

K) Many student cooperate with faculty in their research work. Faculty does highly intensive research and students get a better grip on those subjects working with them. In addition, many faculty include students' names also in research paper to encourage them which helps a lot in students' career. Students connected with research get special importance in the industry. Thus, it is also very useful initiative which students should adopt.

L) Specialization and its electives must be selected with full consciousness as per own interest after due consideration and consulting others. Summer internship's company and project given by it should be carefully chosen according to specialization as all this has direct connection with placement and future career.

□

7
Summer Internship

During two year course, at the end of the third trimester often in April end, students are sent for summer internships. As stated earlier, the summer internship is of at least eight weeks duration and during this period students have to join some company and work on the subject assigned by them and at a place assigned by them. A company can ask students to work on some immediate problems in company. For example, if a particular product is not being sold in the market, then company would like to know about the reasons for the same and this problem is assigned to students as a project. Similarly, if a company wants to know the training needs of its employees then it may assign this as another project to students for doing company employees' survey. This project comes under HR Department whereas the first project falls in marketing or sales department. In finance area, students may be assigned to survey product production and potential reduction in costs.

In whole programme, this is the first opportunity for students when they see face-to-face real situations and where they connect with any industry or company in reality. Through summer internship, they get first chance to go in a company themselves and connect with their system and activities. Working together with company professionals and departmental experts, they get to learn new things and in parallel they also understand practical applications of subjects and concepts taught in the class. Students also get guidance from their faculty on these projects and they are explained which particular tools and concepts of a given subject can be used to solve the given problem.

It is necessary for students to give lot of importance to summer internships and complete the work assigned by the company with full honesty and dedication. Be in regular touch with company's professionals and experts and take their guidance. Also be in contact of their faculty. On one hand, result of good work is to gain knowledge and skills, on the other hand, it helps in better placement in future. Many companies offer placement to students based upon their excellent work, working style and acquired knowledge, which is called pre-placement offer. In pre-placement offer student's job is guaranteed and student may join that company after completion of the course. A company has to confirm in writing of such an offer. A student can also sit in other companies' placement process not accepting the pre-placement offer. Getting pre-placement offer for its students is a matter of pride for any institution and students also take pride in this. In IIMs, pre-placement offers are in abundance and therefore they have very good image.

After studying the problem assigned in summer internships, students have to submit a written report and make a presentation before the company, wherein the company's professionals and experts evaluate their work. While they evaluate student's work on one side, on the other side, they also discuss how the students' findings and recommendations could be implemented in the company. Depending upon usefulness of students' work for the company, that work is ranked. According to the rules of the institutions, company has to submit its evaluation to the institution and company's marks are combined with marks allotted by the institute and based upon cumulative score of the two, students' summer internship results are declared. Normally, total sum of its marks is 100 or 200. As per institute's rules, students have to submit a written report after coming back from summer internship and have to make a power point presentation based upon which institute allot them marks. Along with this students have to submit a certificate given by the company's guide (professional/expert) in which the guide certify that particular student has done satisfactory student work and his work has been accepted by the company.

Based upon summer internships, many students write research paper or cases jointly with their faculty which is quite beneficial for students' careers. During this period, Summer Internship Competitions are organized by various institutions in which students must participate. Students reaching in the final round of such competitions are rewarded based upon their presentation and quiz rounds which have considerable value in the industry too. In these competitions, students have to give details of their project and based on the quality of those projects, they are selected for final round where after the presentation first, second, and third winners are declared. Apart from IIMs and other leading institutions nowadays such competitions are also organized by AIHA, AIMA, NHRD, etc. Media channel like CNBC also organizes such competition.

Some other important tips related to summer internships are given below:

1. Students must choose their specialization before summer internship for which necessary details have already been given earlier.
2. After determination of specialization, i.e. marketing, finance, HR, etc. students should sit for selection in companies providing projects in these areas.
3. Company interview students for internships and

they choose students based upon their performance in the interview.

4. Students must be well-prepared for interview both related to subjects knowledge and related to company and industry too.
5. After selecting and joining the company, learn as much as possible related to the assigned project.
6. Based on study and guidance of company's experts and faculty, a project synopsis has to be prepared in which details of company, objective of the project, its methodology, tools to be used have to be given. This works as guidelines for further work.
7. During summer internship project, students from other institutions are also selected for same or the other projects with whom students should work in harmony and interact with them more and more. Such networks prove very useful in future career.
8. Students must keep in mind not to neglect summer internship in any manner and neither they should try to get fake certificate or project through any acquaintances. If caught, not only institution takes strict disciplinary action including expulsion from the course, but students also lose golden opportunity for learning, which is not helpful for their placement too. Many students take such wrong steps and rest at home which is totally wrong. Neither students should do it nor should their parents encourage them to do so.

□

8
Multidimensional Personality

In management career, there is a big demand of holistic personality. Holistic personality means a personality which is not only efficient in studies and has passed with good grade but a personality which has practical skills, confidence, good communication skills, ability to be a team player, have skills to convince people with his words and can carry people along. A personality, who doesn't lose patience in adverse or difficult conditions, doesn't get afraid of difficult situations and has ability to take right decisions. A light-hearted, cheerful person who comes forward to overcome difficulties of others is always welcome.

All these aspects of the personality are not found in a person nor anybody get them through legacy. Some parts of these qualities come with age and experience but there are many qualities which ripe only when one faces such circumstances or if one gets chance to try out these skills or qualities. In industry or corporate world circumstances, such qualities are very much required and the professionals who possess these traits succeed in fulfilling their responsibilities and in their career. Companies assess these qualities and traits seriously during placement process and also during their annual appraisal. Those who pass on these quality standards, their career graph goes very high, such people are found to rise very high at their workplace.

Taking into account the facts discussed above, each management institution during the course put efforts to pay attention in developing these traits among students along with regular studies. Along with studies and other initiatives related with studies, each institution pay lot of emphasis on extracurricular activities. Under this, from management festival to sports, from social service to cultural aspects-related programs are organized. Clubs are formed under each specialization whose purpose is to organize programs during the whole year.

Clubs primarily formed are Marketing Club, Finance Club, HR Club, Communication Club, Operations Club and IT Club in which each student is a member of one or more clubs. The principal activities of each club include organizing conclave to discuss social issues, organize guest talk by the industry-experienced professionals, organizing quiz competition, debate competition, etc. In addition, the clubs also publish their magazine, for which entire responsibility including editing to publishing is handled by students. Clubs also form Facebook pages or websites for promoting their club activities. It is worth mentioning here that all these activities are done by students only and students only participate in these activities and programs. Students from other institutions too are invited in many programs resulting in health competition.

Programs like sports and management festival are organized at large scale and it is tried that students of different institutions from across the country participate in the same. Students from dozens of institutions participate in these programs, rather each year, students wait for these programs. Committee is formed to organize these programs and mainly students' members take initiative in their organization. Though college give its contribution, yet these students also organize sponsorship from different companies. In these programs or separately, cultural programs are also organized like singing competition, dance competition, fashion show, band, etc. With collaboration of national-level organization like SPIC-MACAY, programs of leading artists related to singing, dance forms are also organized. A Heritage Walk is also organized in association with same organization wherein students get exposure of our country's history and heritage. SPIC-MACAY also organizes show of old classic movies. Besides this, movie club also hold movie-shows on regular intervals and show the movies related to management or its various aspects. For example, Aamir Khan's movie *Lagaan* is very good example of team building, leadership, crisis management, men-management concepts, etc. which are elaborated in detail by the faculty experts.

In Literature club, students interest develop towards literature and it inspires the students to read novels, fictions, old classics available in library so that not only their thinking prowess and imagination increase but also their writing and communication skills also improve further. This club often organizes programs like Book Review, etc. and reward the students whose reviews are found best.

Corporate Responsibility Club (CSR), Entrepreneurship Club, Conference Club, International Relations Club are few other clubs whose activities are of great importance and students get huge benefits through their organization and through participation in the same. CSR Club organizes social or social welfare-related programs. For example, plantation program, health check-up program, eye check-up camps, blood donation camps, special programs for poor children on Independence Day or Republic Day, and collaboration with NGO for various other social work. From these activities, awareness and responsibility towards society develops among students which motivate them to do similar work in their future corporate life.

Entrepreneurship Club plays a key role in today's context. From skill development to campus company or beginning of startup, this club plays major role. In programs like 'My Story Session', successful entrepreneurs are called who share their success stories with students which inspire students to become entrepreneur. Students go to various clusters and talk to industries, workers and people who set-up the industries there and understand the nuances of running industries. All this help them in launching their own ventures.

The Conference Club holds a big annual conference and its benefit goes to students organizing it. International Relations Club members, establish contacts of the institute with the foreign universities and institution. Faculty and students exchange programs where foreign students and faculty come to the institute and institute faculty and students go there is mainly organized by this club members only. Members of this club or other students who get opportunity to go abroad and see and understand industries there are highly benefitted from such opportunities. Its benefit comes out in form of placement in good companies.

Besides, students also get many other opportunities where they can develop their skills. Discipline committee, academic program committee, placement committee, admission committee, media relation committee, hostel and mess Committee, students welfare committee, in all these committees students can work as members and play important role in proper functioning of the institution. These are all such opportunities where students through active participation can improve their skills, personality and maturity level. This experience helps them during placement. Therefore, students should pay attention that along with good studies they also have to play an active role in extracurricular activities.

□

9

Training and Placement

The important milestone of two year management course is placement that is students getting satisfactory jobs of their own liking in some company. While on one hand it is important for future of the students and is a result of hard work put during two years course, on the other hand, it is equally important for institution that its students are selected by the companies coming for campus placement resulting in establishing credibility of the course and education offered by the institution.

As stated earlier, both domestic and multinational companies come to the institutions each year for selecting and hiring their students. It is as per company's own annual plan, according to which they fulfill human resource needs of its various departments. Companies go for students' selection each year only to the prestigious and reputed institutions, whose students' earlier years' placement records have been satisfactory. Institutions have good relationships with these companies and throughout the whole year it is attempted that students remain connected in one or the other ways with these companies and companies' professionals also remained connected with institution to share their knowledge and experience.

Normally, companies employ the students on post of management trainee during placement and after six months training absorbs students in regular employment. Many other companies recruit as executive also in addition to management trainee. These recruitments are mainly done for marketing, sales, finance, HR, operations and other departments of the company. There are set criteria of each department and it is expected from students to meet knowledge and skills requirements of those criteria. Overall a company look for following qualities in a student:

- Information about surrounding and global environment especially related to economy, trade, political and community.
- Along with information about these activities and conditions, capability of analyzing and putting forward own opinion and further to keep own point of view on any issue.
- Knowledge of related subjects especially of the subjects of the department where student is likely to be selected. What is the relationship of those subjects with departmental functions and how those can be put to practical use, a mature understanding is required on these issues.
- Communication style and capabilities are largely expected. It is mandatory to speak correct in good style. Special attention is paid towards how meticulously one can put forward his issues and how meaningful are the contents of one's words.
- Companies also pay special attention towards how confidence is reflected from one's personality, values of the student and if he is honest in his words and deeds or not.
- It is also evaluated very minutely how a student behavior and response is in some particular situations particularly under pressure.

During placement, first of all company informs that in which departments it require students and many a time it also informs how many students are required. In each department what are the responsibilities expected at each position, detailed description of the same is given by the companies to the institution which is shared with students. Then company informs about date of their visit to the institution. On that date, first of all company gives a pre-placement talk to students and inform them once again about the company, position and about the work and package. Only those students sit in the pre-placement talk who are interested in that company based upon information already shared. After pre-placement talk, company starts selection process which is completed in many rounds. These mainly consisted of aptitude test, GD and personal interview.

The company opts for selection process from these two or three rounds. After the whole day process, company informs the institution names of selected students and institution inform the students either simultaneously or within the time-limit prescribed as per institution rules. Some companies shortlist the students and hold their final round with their senior officer or panel. In that case name of selected students are declared after final round. Each institution has some rules and norms for placement which each student has to adhere to. All students are required to sign an undertaking in this regard and a student who do not follow the rules is debarred from the placement process. Generally, after selection and declaration of his name in a company placement process, a student is not allowed to sit in any other company placement process. Student has to join that company only where his selection has already been done. Still, in many institutions, if a company is offering very high package and if an already selected student is eligible for that company then he is given a chance for that company also. On the other hand, if a student has given his name to sit in a company placement process based upon his eligibility and then doesn't take part in the process upon company visit, then placement committee takes action against him. If no satisfactory reason is found, then student is debarred from further placement process due to his absence. Similarly, it is also mentioned in placement guidelines that what percentage of attendance is required for the training arranged related to placement. A student must know how much attendance in class is required and what is the minimum percentage of marks (CGPA) required. On one hand, he must know the whole placement process, on the other hand, he needs to put full efforts in preparation for placement process. It is necessary to understand following points in context of placement preparation:

1. First of all, students must prepare their bio data (CV) after returning back from summer internship by the end of Term 4. There are many formats (templates) to prepare CV, one of which is given in Appendix 2. In this CV, along with personal information, full academic details must be given. Other important information like specialization, topic of summer internships and other details, various projects done during course, participation in different competitions and special achievements should be mentioned. Also, details related to extra-curricular activities and one's hobbies should also be given. Note that no wrong or false information should be given in CV and student should be able to convince the panel members for all the information given in CV. A CV is reflection of any student, therefore, full attention must be paid on this.
2. As has been said before, students must decide their specialization and its related subjects before going for summer internship. After that they should regularly study all these subjects with full dedication till the placement time approaches. Even among core

subjects, those related to specialization or related to a particular job should be specially studied. While studying students must have full grip on knowledge about main concepts and their practical applications. For this purpose, faculty organizes separate special classes for main concept and their applications which not only helps in revision but also strengthen the application side of the concepts learnt. Students get its advantages during placement interview, i.e. personal interview. Students must pay full attention to this.

3. Questions are asked in details about summer internship during personal interview, therefore following points should specially be kept in mind:
   (i) Topic of summer internship
   (ii) Specific reason to choose the topic and main findings at the end of project, which are expected
   (iii) Detailed information about the company and industry
   (iv) Project methodology – concepts of methodology
   (iv) Concepts of subjects related to the project
   (vi) Benefit to company from the findings at the end of the project
   (vii) Learning and benefits from the project.

Students should prepare answers for all these points in advance in which they can take help of their faculty guide. Always, practice answers to these questions during mock interview. A brief note of two-three pages should be handy that helps in revision.

At the beginning of the placement process, many companies take the aptitude test and based upon this test result, companies shortlist 10-20 percent or more students for next round. A very large percentage of students are eliminated in this round itself. Therefore, it is necessary that students perform well in this round and cross this hurdle to participate in next round of GD and personal interview. The aptitude test is not a new thing for students as they prepare for same type of questions for their MBA enrollment process also for which details have already been given. quantitative analysis, reasoning, comprehensive, and situation analysis, etc. are included in the aptitude test. It is essential for students to practice these well and solve the model test papers of the same. Institution organize special training classes for this purpose and students should take benefit of the same. This test is not so difficult that a student can't pass it. Generally, it is seen that due to lack of practice, students are not able to clear this. Therefore, right preparation and regular practice is the root of success for this round.

4. Current affairs, which contains details of industry, company, economy and activities or incidences happening all around the globe, is a very important aspect of personal interview round of placement on which students must focus on. Note that these issues cannot be prepared or learnt in a few days. For this it is desirable that students start paying attention to immediately after joining the course if they have not done in past. For this, it is necessary to bear in mind few points:
   (i) Read daily newspaper. A general and a business newspaper. Students should develop their understanding and opinion about main news, current happenings or new developments. Library and online resources offer facilities for the same.
   (ii) Consult regularly the websites that provide detailed description of such matters. Nowadays many mobile apps give such information. Students should take their benefit.

(iii) Many discussions happen on TV channels every day, students should regularly watch and listen the ones relevant to them and form their views on those subjects.

(iv) Different clubs of the institution organize talks and discussion on currents affairs and relevant topics in which students should participate very actively. These clubs also organize panel discussions arranged by students in which students should participate very actively with full preparation.

(v) Guest sessions related to industry and company are organized by the institution during placement season and students should definitely take their benefits.

(vi) It is also necessary for students that they discuss on these issues at their level at their own or in groups and prepare notes of the main points. Industry and company-related information can also be collected and distributed in group. This will result in collecting lot of information about different companies and industries by a small number of students.

Mock interviews are arranged by institution faculty and industry experts for preparing for personal interviews so that students may know their strengths and weaknesses. Students should take advantage of these mock sessions. Do video recording of these sessions, watch later and improve upon weaknesses. Observe minutely from communication style to body language and try to improve by taking opinion of faculty and other experts. It is an important initiative for placement preparation. Many videos are available on you-tube related to art and style of personal interviews and students should take their benefit too. In addition, faculty of business communication also give many suggestions and organize separate classes for students of which students should take advantage. Students should practice for mock interview in groups whenever they get a chance in hostel or in institution.

Group discussion is also an important round of placement process which happens before the personal interview. Students are required to be successful in this round, then only they can go to the next round. Full details relating to the preparation of group discussions has already been given in detail in earlier chapter related to nomination, therefore, there is no justification for repeating the same here. Students should prepare for group discussions as per suggested ways and participate in group discussion.

During personal interviews, many such questions are asked from the students whose answers should be given in affirmation and with honesty. For example, why does a student want to join a particular company or why does he want to do a particular job. Company asks question related to job location from students. In today's age, when all facilities are available in small and big cities, commuting facilities are available and company also equally focuses on small and big cities and nearer or distant cities then students should not hesitate to work at any location. There are many such small but important points that students must take care of. Institutions also give tips related to these points during training.

To summarize, it can be said that students can succeed with very good placement by putting hard work during two years and by paying attention to above suggested points and implementing them. Students must pay heed to these details so that both their future and career shine brightly.

□

10
Experts Opinion

In earlier pages, I have put efforts to share in nutshell my experiences on different aspects in which all those points are covered which are necessary for a student to reach his destination of MBA. From here onwards, in next section, I have tried to share the opinion and experiences of some special, experienced, well-known experts of the country. All experts have discussed, how the economy is presently, how it is expected to move in future and what the prospects are for a MBA in this economic scenario. In today's industry, what areas and what type of opportunities are available there and what type of MBAs are required by them has also been discussed. How to study for MBA and prepare for placement and what are the things to be kept in mind, experiences have been shared on all these points by the experts for different sectors. No wonder that a harmony can be seen in suggestions of all experts and they are on same track about putting efforts and direction of preparation. In this section, it is also described how to choose a right B-school and how to prepare for enrollment process. All experts have emphasized strongly on how a MBA should contribute in society and nation building along with his work.

Readers are requested to read all interviews minutely, understand the points explained there and follow the given suggestions.

□

Values like Honesty, Integrity, Passion and Initiative have High Premium in Industry

1. What prospects/opportunities you see for an MBA in today's scenario.

Dr. H. Chaturvedi
Director
Birla Institute of Management Technology,
Greater Noida

Management courses are offered in wide range of disciplines. Management covers courses in major areas such as marketing, human resources/ organizational behaviour and strategic management, etc. Teaching in these courses is drawn on a range of disciplines, which include mathematics, psychology, sociology, philosophy and economics. The ideas and practices from these diverse disciplines are applied to the understanding and management of voluntary, commercial and public sector organizations.

Education in management has two aims. Firstly, to increase the understanding of the factors which influence the conduct of organizations and secondly to provide students with the tools and techniques which they may use to influence organizational life.

Why pursue an MBA?

- To launch a progressive career
- To make a shift in career, if you already are an experienced professional
- To nurture an innovative outlook
- To network with the best in the market
- To add a brand value to yourself
- To enhance personal growth
- To start a business/start-up/turn entrepreneur
- To move geographically

2. **How to prepare for MBA Entrance exams?**

   MBA is one of the most sought-after careers in the current scenario around the world. As a result preparation for MBA entrance exams is equally hectic and tough. The mother of all MBA entrance exams is CAT, scores of which are used for admission to the IIMs. MBA preparation and CAT preparation requires months of hard work and dedication.

   CAT preparation is done well only if you follow a rigorous mock test regime. Mock tests are the most important part of CAT prep in my opinion. You can attend all classes and cover all study material but it is all for nothing if you don't take mocks. Start with one full length test and a couple of sectional tests a week and increase that to two full length tests and two sectional tests each three months prior to CAT and stop taking mocks 20 days before the D-day. Other than that, identify your weaknesses and work on them, but make yourself best at your strengths. That is where mocks come in handy. Analyze each test you take and identify what went wrong and where you do consistently well.

   To clear the examination a student will require in-depth knowledge, analytical mind, sharp memory and above all, systematic planning and preparation.

Needless to say, that the aspirants should not attempt to prepare for their MBA Entrance Test overnight. Even though syllabus in the admission/ entrance test is the same such as CAT, XAT, MAT, CMAT, SNAP, etc., it does not differ from university to university. These aspects include tests on quantitative aptitude, reasoning, intelligence, comprehension, case analysis, relationships, word power, synonyms, antonyms, general knowledge/ awareness, etc.

3. **How to Select a B School?**

There are 1000-plus B-schools in India and half a dozen rankings to boot; notwithstanding the numerous claims and counter-claims in the print and/or electronic media. All of these seem to be true at first sight but it really is a Hobson's choice to decide which one to select and which one to prune out from the wannabe list. Following is an exhaustive list of governing parameters in order of importance, for a student to decide the B-school best suited to his/her interests and competence. The governing parameters have been grouped as PRIMARY and SECONDARY:

Primary Parameters	Secondary Parameters
1. Industry Interface	1. Degree Vs Diploma
2. Pedagogy and Strength of course	2. Boarding Vs Day School Programme
3. Faculty	3. Global affiliations and accreditations
4. Alumni Strength	4. Fee Structure
5. Specialized B-schools	5. Location
6. Placements	6. Timing of entrance examination
7. Infrastructure	

8. Research Excellence Vs Academic Excellence.	

4. **Job opportunities after an MBA.**

Every MBA wants to see a return on their investment. Going to business school can boost your career prospects, and in many industries having an MBA will give you the edge over competition. After falling from 2008, applications for MBA admission rose in 2012, according to the Graduate Management Admission Council.

With more B-school students entering MBA programs, selecting the right career path becomes important for current MBAs and alumni. With more MBAs entering the workforce, pursuing the right field can ensure your career progression.

While an undergraduate BA might get you started, many companies want someone with an MBA, especially in certain industries. These are five jobs where an MBA can make you more attractive to employers and help give you an edge in the MBA jobs market.

IT Manager

IT managers oversee a company's computer systems. That can mean ensuring computer systems meet a company's needs, upgrading technology and keeping the system secure. It also frequently includes managing IT personnel.

Companies want managers with IT experience, sometimes in a lower-level management position. MBAs have the management experience to lead an IT team, with the skills to deal with executives. MBA graduates who stay ahead of the latest technological innovations will have an improved chance of employment.

Financial Manager

Finance is a great match for MBAs because it is a field that closely aligns with graduate education. Financial managers oversee a company's financial condition, preparing or reviewing financial reports, analysing trends and advising the top management personnel on finances and profits.

Many companies want financial managers with an MBA, as these candidates tend to have the analytical abilities and software knowledge required to do the ob. Experience in finance industry will naturally help.

Financial Advisor

Another finance-job that seeks out MBA graduates is that of financial advisor. Financial advisors provide investment, retirement, tax and insurance guidance for clients, including financial goals or investment strategies. An MBA could help financial advisors attract clients. For those who are not self-employed, an MBA can make it easier to move into a management role.

HR Manager

Increasing demands on human resources departments drives the need for skilled HR managers. This position directs administrative action for an entire company and works on recruiting and hiring for an organization. Experience and an MBA can open advancement into this position, as HR managers work closely with executives and participate in strategic planning.

Management Analyst

Management analysts recommend improvements to companies on costs, personnel, finances, alternate practices or work on solving specific problems. About 23 percent are self-employed.

The disciplines and knowledge you gain from an MBA strongly increases your chances to enter any of these fields and unlocks the path for advancement, especially when coupled with a few years of experience. If you are looking for MBA jobs, these five industries are a good place to start.

5. **How you think an MBA can contribute towards society and nation building?**

Creation of an inclusive society is essentially facing three challenges: poverty, education and sustainable development. Poverty is posing an imposing challenge in creation of an inclusive society. It deprives people from even the basic needs of food and shelter. Poverty thereby leads them being automatically excluded from the mainstream. This can be solved by creation of more employment opportunities. MBA students can venture into entrepreneurship to solve this problem of poverty. Efforts in the form of vocational training can be made to make these people self-sufficient which will increase the self-confidence of these people thus enabling them to be an active member of the society. Education also plays an important part in bring about equity in the society. People who are educated can take informed decisions and also put forth their views about issues affecting them. MBA students can devote some part of their time during the time they are pursuing their education as well as after they have completed to teaching under-privileged children.

MBA students, once they become mangers, also have the responsibility to run their business sustainably. They will have to realize that they need to preserve resources for the generations to come. They will also have to be careful about ensuring that they preserve the environment and work in collaboration with people are bound to get affected by their work to ensure their development and wellness.

Thus, MBA students will have to identify and create strategies and programmes that will have an impact on the urgent social and ecological problems and make a positive contribution towards shaping an inclusive society.

6. **Besides skills and knowledge, what kind of values you would look for in an MBA?**

   Honesty – Whatever ethical plane you hold yourself to, when you are responsible for a team of people, it's important to raise the bar even higher. Your business and its employees are a reflection of yourself, and if you make honest and ethical behavior a key value, your team will follow.

   Passion – Passion is a useful tool for staying motivated and productive, whether it's in school or business. But it goes much deeper than simply being passionate about what you are doing. You need to express your passion in a way that will inspire and project energy onto those you are working with.

   Integrity – Integrity is more than being respectful. It's more than any single attribute. Integrity is a combination of attributes, "Integrity" that make up this value: creates trust, unafraid of reality, results oriented, solves negative realities, causes growth, and finds meaning in life.

   Initiative – You need to demonstrate the desire and ability to spark up a new conversation or idea. Any situation in which you took charge voluntarily, rather than being assigned something.

7. **What are the tips for MBA aspirants coming from relatively smaller towns and those whose medium of teaching has been Hindi?**

English is not really as big a monster as people tell you it is. The first step in solving a problem is identifying the problem. Don't cram new words. Work on the basics of grammar first, then, while trying to expand your vocabulary, do it methodologically. Maintain a notebook. When you see a new word, write it down, write a sentence explaining its usage, a few synonyms and antonyms, a few words with the same root word (if any) or belonging to the same family (food, animals, etc.). Work on it like it is a strategy-based game. As for accent, it only comes when you start talking to people in English and shed away the fear. Start by talking out loud to yourself in the mirror. It is all very clichéd but if people laugh at your mistakes, use that as motivation for becoming better.

□

Huge Opportunities await in E-Commerce, Banking, Financial Sector & Others

1. **What prospects/opportunities you see for an MBA in today's scenario.**

Dr. D.P. Goyal
Dean
MDI, Gurgaon

The basic objective of a typical MBA programme is to help students to understand social, economic, ecological environment of modern global society and its characteristic values so that they become effective leaders who may achieve results beyond expectations and transform organisations to meet the global challenges.

In today's scenario of ever-increasing global competitiveness coupled with information explosion, there are ample prospects and opportunities for MBAs to prove that they have the abilities and capabilities to bring about the much-desired transformation in the business organisations. To exploit these opportunities, they need to equip themselves with all the capabilities so as to achieve more with less; more quickly; and more uniquely.

2. **What are the prospects for a fresh MBA in different sectors?**

A fresh MBA has an important role to play in all the sectors like retail, e-commerce, manufacturing, banking & financial sector, real estate, e-governance, software services, IT infrastructure, etc.

3. **What are the qualities you look in an MBA when you go for recruitments?**

   An MBA should have fundamental knowledge of management, global business environment, functional areas of management and positive mindset coupled with an excellent communication.

4. **How you think an MBA can contribute towards society and nation building?**

   The society is looking towards ethical and sustainable practices of the business organisations at large. The MBAs can really contribute by leading the organisations with value based and sustainable management practices. The strong character of MBAs can help building a strong nation.

5. **What are the tips for MBA aspirants coming from relatively smaller towns and those whose medium of teaching has been Hindi?**

   The students coming from relatively smaller towns and those whose medium of teaching has been Hindi, are required to get themselves sufficiently exposed with the requirements to get admission in a good MBA programme. They need to have all the initiative and will to overcome the weaknesses so that they are confident. If they are good in content and able to convey the message, communication may not be a big challenge for success. Moreover, communication and confidence can be improved with practice.

6. **What kind of preparation an aspirant should do for getting into a good B-school**

   A prospective student for a good B-school needs

to have verbal, reasoning, quantitative and data interpretation abilities. Thus, an aspirant must prepare accordingly and practice through mock tests and interviews. Also speed of attempting questions needs to be improved to get competitive advantage.

7. **How should an aspirant select a good B-school?**

   An aspirant of a good B-school should focus on the quality of governance of the school, quality of its faculty, pedagogy of delivery, alumni base, infrastructure (like library databases and computer software), opportunities for international exposure and live projects, the type of companies visiting for guest lectures and for recruiting students and the compensation package offerings.

8. **Besides skills and knowledge, what kind of values you would look for in an MBA?**

   The recruiters want an MBA should be having a high integrity, positive mindset, innovative abilities and effective communication to handle business problems.

□

Opportunities lie Ahead in Technology Development and Other New Sectors

1. **What prospects/opportunities do you see for an MBA in today's scenario?**

Dr. Kamna Malik
Professor & Consultant
Director
KLM Associates
New Delhi
Adjunct Professor – IT
GlobalNxt University,
Malaysia

Need for a general manager and administrator is ever green and is across the industry verticals. However, greater opportunities lie ahead for those who embrace technology, can think and understand unconventional business and outsourcing models, and visualize abstract patterns of data. While the likes of Google, Paytm and Uber have touched the masses through consumerization of IT, brick and mortar businesses like automotive, banking, insurance and real estate are also embarking on new horizons through web and Internet of things. It's an era of convergence, so prospects for an individual will no longer be constrained to one industry. Mobility across industries is going to be much easier and frequent.

2. **What are the prospects for a fresh MBA in IT and education and other sectors?**
In addition to routine jobs in various business functions, fresh MBAs can look out for upcoming entry level jobs in the areas of social marketing, mobility, cloud and big data analytics. These jobs exist in all kinds of industries, including outsourcing companies. With content creation, skills training, education management and skills assessments emerging as distinct business lines, there is a lot that fresh and seasoned MBAs can bring to the table in various roles related to student mobilization, institutional linkages, talent management, digitization and overall project / program management etc. In addition, the time is ripe for more and more MBAs to get entrepreneurial.
3. **What are the qualities you look in an MBA when you go for recruitments?**
I look for individuals who are aspiring yet grounded, theoretically sound yet practical. Some of the key skills that I expect them to have are – reading, writing and presentation skills, critical and analytical thinking, customer centricity, problem solving, team work, attention to detail and ability to plan, organize and decide. Other stuff can be taught but these skills are like the root.
4. **What specific things that an MBA should do to make a sound career in industry while studying?**
First and foremost – feel and behave as an effective manager. Next, do what you enjoy and enjoy what you do.
If you still enjoy bunking classes, bullying a peer who asks questions, updating your Facebook/ Whatsapp status while the class is on, chances are high that you are far off from being a manager.

Come forward, take charge, ask, explore, discuss, share and collaborate to make your surroundings a place to be in. A place where positive thoughts and actions flourish.

5. **How an MBA should groom himself/herself for a better career path after joining industry?**

   Join a company not for its brand but for the value you can co-create. Avoid job hops for a meager salary hike. Hop, if at all, for a more challenging and forward looking role.

   As you go up the ladder, you need to have more diverse skill set. So, maintain reading as your hobby and join professional circles, LinkedIn groups for example. Aim to balance the depth and breadth of your skills, e.g. if you are a marketing person, you ought to remain updated on marketing tools and techniques; but also get updated on allied areas like finance, supply chain and people management.

   Set high standards for yourself and be your own competitor. (Competing with others brings restlessness, so stay safe.) Keep a watch on the professional trends. Many countries publish career paths and talent demand patterns. India is also working towards setting up its workforce management information system, connecting various industry bodies and the skilling ecosystem. India's skills building initiative is also working towards recognition of prior learning, which will give boost to on-the-job training, up-skilling and mobility up and across the career paths.

6. **How is IT industry and industry in general looking up for future, say next five years?**

   Though the trends are generally positive, markets are increasingly becoming vulnerable and unpredictable owing to increasing technical, social and natural upheavals. Nevertheless, emphasis on globalization, mechanization, digitization and service orientation is bound to increase. This will mean immense pressure on individuals and companies for performance and more frequent acquisitions, mergers and transformations. Mobility and Internet of things is going to be the way to work. While on one side, technology stands the chance to eat up routine jobs, a dearth of quality work force, quick learners and specialists is equally being felt across the board.

7. **Besides skills and knowledge, what kind of values you would look for in an MBA?**

   They should be human first. Have peace, trust, honesty, love, empathy and respect for nature and living beings.

   Perhaps, we have started believing that knowledge and skills are only related to a job occupation. Values also come with knowledge and skills. They actually originate from knowledge and skills of life; and business values should be no different than human and social values. Companies today make policies to recognize loyalty and service excellence; and penalize dishonesty. That's an indication of reducing human values that need to be restored. Otherwise, what is honesty, loyalty and service excellence if it's not hundred percent?

   Had it not been lack of honesty and trust, I believe, Indian employers would have long offered flexi work hours or work from home options for many jobs and Delhi would not have been crying for a car free day and even-odd car days.

8. **How do you think an MBA can contribute towards society and nation building?**

By being happy and positive in one's thoughts and actions. By virtue of their job profile, MBAs are a catalyst for business and economic growth. Unfortunately social divide, pollution, stress and time poverty are some of the costs that come along with this growth. MBAs need to think radical and find ways for inclusive and holistic socio-economic growth. They can create more jobs and happy work place for others.

9. **What are the tips for MBA aspirants coming from relatively smaller towns and those whose medium of teaching has been Hindi?**

   Neither small town, nor Hindi medium is a constraint for the ones who believe in themselves. Think of PM Modi or Google Chief Sundar Pichai. Life is all about learning and unlearning. Go an extra mile to attend a short-term course or click a link to a free online course. If you decide to step ahead and take charge of your own self, nothing is unachievable.

□

Industry Demands Multifaceted Abilities and Skills in a Manager

1. **How an MBA should groom himself/herself for a better career path after joining industry?**

Richa Dhar
Consultant
Training and Placement

Getting the first job is always a difficult process. Students spend the two years of their MBA preparing for a campus placement. But to be able to retain one's first job and to succeed is even more difficult. A lot of times students especially freshers, leave their first job within the first year. Reasons can be anything ranging from target pressure, to location. Most of the times, this frustration van be avoided if they prepare themselves for a life after MBA.

Ideally, the preparation for a career after joining the industry should start form the first year of MBA. Students should undergo, training on Gaol setting, career counselling and self-development.

Also the colleges should try and provide the students with opportunities to meet managers and CEOs from different industries for getting a clear understanding on the Industries expectations from them.

In addition to this given below are the eight things that an MBA graduate should work on along with job preparation:

(i) **Choose an industry that matches his/her skills:** This is the most important advice for an MBA student. It not only helps them perform better in job interviews, but is also important to develop career clarity. Choosing the right industry that matches their personality or interest will save a lot of heart burn to them and to the company as well. Students should research about the industry, the work life in that industry. They should also talk to their alumni in that industry to understand the work culture and the skill requirement.

(ii) **Develop an in-depth knowledge of the industry:** Once they have finalised the industry of their choice, the second step should be to develop an in-depth knowledge of the industry and the job role.

Technical knowledge and business awareness are two things that help a person perform better.

(iii) **Develop strong communication skills:** Ability to communicate your ideas and present them to the senior management or the client is crucial to the success of an individual. Managerial communication skills reflect on the professionalism of a person. Good communication skills are essential for the managers irrespective of the industry or the job role.

(iv) **Learn business networking:** Networking is an important skill. Unfortunately, this is not stressed enough in the management colleges. Students need to develop their own network/ connections with people in the similar industry. They need to connect with their alumni, attend seminars and workshops to meet industry people also. LinkedIn is a very important platform, which the students should be trained on using effectively.

(v) **Develop public speaking and presentation skills:** Although these are usually clubbed with communication skills, yet Public speaking and communication skills need a separate mention. For most of the students, designing effective PPT or to present their ideas in front of a group of people is a nerve-racking experience. Unfortunately, this has become an unavoidable part of every manager's role, especially those dealing with clients.

Students would be introduced to public speaking clubs like Toastmasters International and should be provided training in the same. The class group presentations are not very effective as the shy students usually hide behind others. This is training that each student should receive individually.

(vi) **Learn business etiquette:** Etiquette in a business environment is different than that in a school, college or home. The difference is something that most of the MBA graduates are not aware of. MBA schools spend majority of focus on interview etiquette, which is important, but how to handle real life situations once on the job, is an experience that leaves most of the students, bewildered lost in their jobs. It is also a major reason why most of them are not able to perform or adjust in their new work environment.

(vii) **Develop time management and organisational skills:** Multitasking is a skill companies look for in managers. Also, unlike in colleges where the deadlines are flexible, in organisations they are sacrosanct. In addition to being able to perform within the limited timelines and resources, it is also important that these young managers have impressive organisational skills. Being resourceful and able to work in teams, handle crisis and deliver quality work, is a skill that comes with practice and experience. Unfortunately, most often young managers get this experience on in their jobs.

They should work on developing these skills while pursuing their management degree through short-term projects with the industry, summer internship and by participating in various events organised in the college.

(viii) **Should identify his/her weaknesses and work on them:** SWOT is tool that can help the management students, get a true picture of their, strengths and areas of improvements. Also, a SWOT followed by a career counselling sessions will help the students to identify the industry and job most suitable for them. A timely SWOT will also help them develop an individual development plan with strict timelines for self-improvement.

It is important that colleges also realise that merely imparting information on management topics will not help their students in long term. Teaching through case studies and short-term project son the real industry can help these students; build a stronger understanding of the real life business scenarios.

In order, for these students to be able to develop a strong career trajectory after joining the industry, it is important that they work on the above-mentioned areas while still in college.

2. **Besides skills and knowledge, what kind of values you would look for in an MBA?**

   Management skills are at the core of any MBA job, but the industry looks for more than a technically smart individual who can achieve targets. Companies look for people who can adjust in the company culture and can add value to the organisation.

   Companies are on the lookout for a potential leader who has high moral character. More and more companies have started including situational questions to judge the moral fibre of the individuals. These can be situations referring to conflict of interest or ability to handle difficult people, etc.

   Companies are interested in hiring people who understand the culture, mission and can work together of the vision. Money and individual growth is important, but organisations refrain from hiring people who want to join them only because of package or brand value. They believe such people are very self-centred and may not stay with the organisation for long.

   Based on my interaction with the managers across the industry following is a short list of the additional values that the companies look for in the individual while hiring:

   (i) **Integrity:** This is a value that the companies are very particular about. They check this through various situational questions. The reality is that there is no right or wrong answer. It depends on what are the priorities of the individual. Training for such questions should include ability to balance between the extremes and a strong set of principles. Primarily, it is the evaluation of the basic fabric of an individual's character. It is important that the candidates work to strengthen their own value system and understand the good businesses need people who can be trusted. They should not try to bluff their way in the interview rather work on making they better human beings.

(ii) **Self-confidence:** This is more of a personality trait. It is the basic requirement for nay job whether corporate or anywhere else. Without confidence even good amount of knowledge will be of no help.

Unfortunately, this is an area where most of our students lack. Belief in your own strengths and potential is extremely important for others to believe in you. In organisations, managers have to deal with difficult people and unexpected situations on daily basis. Self-confidence is important for them to develop handle these daily doses of stress, otherwise they will not be able to survive in this dynamic and competitive world.

(iii) **Emotional intelligence:** Organisations need managers who can lead, work with others, take initiative and can handle tremendous amount of pressure and yet deliver on the expectations. In short, they are looking for people with strong emotional intelligence.

EI mean being aware of your own emotions

and able to understand that of others. Such people can control their own temper are very good at handling conflicts, difficult people, negotiating contracts, handling stress and working with teams. In fact, this is a very important character trait to become a leader.

(iv) **Ability to work hard and smart:** The age-old value of hard work has never diminished. It is one of the important values that companies look for in the fresh recruits. In addition to the hard work, the companies also want people with creative problem solving and good decision-making ability clubbed with ability to multitasking. They want people who can handle situations and achieve targets. In short, hard work clubbed with smart work is what companies look for in the potential candidate.

These are some of the basic values that the companies look for in the candidates. Also they want flexible people with positive attitude.

Most of the students have these skills, but it is also important to highlight these during the interviews and then practice them while in the job.

While hiring companies look for people who will stay for a longer duration and could be groomed as the future leaders. Hence, it is important the students work on building a good character, and colleges emphasise on ethics, innovation and creative problem solving to help students develop their Emotional Quotient.

3. **What are the tips for MBA aspirants coming from relatively smaller towns and those whose medium of teaching has been Hindi?**

Requirements of the industry from the MBA students are now more or less defined, with few changes here and there based on the specific job role. The companies look for well-groomed candidates with good communication skills, high ethical values, good technical knowledge and preferably some work experience or industry exposure through internships or projects.

They want candidates with high emotional intelligence and out of the box thinking. Nearly, all of these qualities can be groomed in any candidate who is willing to put that extra effort. The background of the individual does not play much role here.

But the major difference that the students coming from smaller towns face is that of poor English communication skills and grooming. The other area of weakness is usually the low level of exposure to the corporate world.

The challenge of oral and written communication becomes more difficult for the students coming from Hindi medium background.

The colleges need to have a robust training need identification process built into their systems. An early realisation of the communication skills gap will provide the students with sufficient time to improve their spoken and written English skills.

Two years is a not a sufficient time to build someone's English communication skills completely. But these students should focus on some specific areas.

Rather than studying grammar from the start, they need to work on topics like tenses, sentence construction, articles, verb forms, etc. Also they should work on building strong writing skills especially writing an email, resume, reports, letters, queries, etc.

With regard to spoken English, they need to participate in as many activities as possible where they will get a chance to speak in English. The colleges should provide such students with mentors, who can help them in developing these skills and can work with them in identifying the level of progress.

The next area to work upon for these students should be to work on as many live project as possible. Working with different organisations will give them a good understanding of what is corporate culture, how to communicate, and what are the company's expectations from them.

The summer internship is another area where they should focus. They need to create a good quality report, as it will help them during their interview.

The last thing these candidates should do is intensive Group discussion and mock interview practices, as these will help them create language flow to answer the standard questions, develop a better understanding of their strengths and weaknesses. Also it will help them develop their confidence levels.

All the above-mentioned activities in addition to the reading regular newspapers and books in English will help them develop their knowledge base, confidence, and English communication skills.

4. **What kind of preparation an aspirant should do for getting into a good B-school? How should an aspirant select a good B-school?**

MBA has become a ticket to a successful career in the corporate. A dream that a lot of young people and their parents nurture. But a mere MBA degree will not help these young minds to achieve their goals. They need to focus on what kind of role are they looking for? How can they achieve it? Is MBA the right option and if yes, which college? The biggest question is in case I do not make it to a top MBA college, how I will choose the best option among the host of colleges claiming 100 percent placements and sky rocketing salaries?

The first question is how to select a good MBA college? They all claim good placements, sate of the art facilities and your dream salary packages. Rather than getting lost on the marketing gimmicks of these colleges or merely choosing where your friend is going to go to or your coaching institute recommends you should conduct your own research.

The first thing to do is to find somebody who has studied there. Search the alumni through LinkedIn, Facebook, etc. Speak to them. They will give you the real picture of the quality of teaching, the industry exposure, the average package, and the recruiters that visit the campus, other hidden costs, if any. For students travelling from different cities and especially for girl candidates, safety should also be kept in mind.

The next thing to do is to check the ranking of the school given by various agencies. Some of the good sources would be Hindustan Times, People Matters, and NHRDN, etc.

A lot of colleges give PGDM or MBA degree, but do not have mandatory recognition. It is important that you check whether the college is recognised or not. Otherwise, a lot of companies will not accept your qualifications. In case, an institute is providing an MBA degree, look for the UGC recognition. You can check the same on the college as well as UGC website. For the colleges offering PGDM, check whether they are recognised by AICTE, also they should be NAAC and NBA Accredited.

Once this is confirmed, check on the list of companies that recruit from the campus. Also confirm what kind of roles these companies hire for. This will help you identify the USP of that college and also if they can help you get a job in the industry and area of specialisation of your choice.

You should always visit the campus before the admission process and meet the faculty, placement manager and talk to the existing students.

These steps will help you identify a college that can prepare you for the role that you aspire.

5. **How to prepare for getting into a good B-school?**

Getting into a good B-school is as difficult as getting a good job. You need to prepare yourself accordingly. Find out the selection criteria for the college. Some colleges take their separate tests like XLRI; some take the score of CAT/MAT. Some institutes shortlist candidates based on their CAT/MAT score and then conduct their own selection process.

Usually, the process includes, case studies, group discussions, written test and one or two rounds of personal interviews.

It is because of this multi-level selection process that preparation of getting into a good B-school cannot happen overnight. One should start working on it from the beginning of the final year of graduation.

Good thing is that the help is available everywhere in the form of various coaching institutes. Select an institute that has proven results for the college/s of your choice. These institutes will help you prepare for all the rounds. But the first focus should be on getting a good score in the CAT, MAT or another test that the school of your choice considers. In order to get into a reputed college you will need a score of at least 85-90 percentiles.

Once you have crossed this hurdle, the next step usually is a GD or a written test. For a good performance in either or both, you need to have good general awareness about issues related to business, society, politics, the world, etc.

Having information alone is not sufficient you also need to have your own point of view or opinion. It will help you present your analytical and creative thinking ability.

For the personal interview, prepare yourself for questions like why MBA? What is of your interest in business? Where do you see yourself five years from now? Why this college? etc.

You will be able to handle these questions only if you have clarity of thought and a good understanding of your own strengths and weaknesses.

Remember that a school can only help you with getting the right set of skills and opportunities; it cannot guarantee a successful career. It is important that you have clarity on why you think MBA is the right option for you, why have you chosen the specialisation you have?

MBA may provide the opportunities for a successful career, but it needs a lot of hard work, choice of the right college and right specialisation. It is where you invest two years and a huge amount of money, hence you should decide the college considering all facts and pursue the course responsibly and then leave no stone unturned in reaching your goal.

□

High Demand for Managing Customers in FMCG and Media Industries

1. **What prospects/opportunities you see for an MBA in today's scenario?**

Mr. Himanshu Manglik
Ex. National Head Corporate Communication
Nestle India

A good grounding in management studies will always open doors. The industry is looking for professionals who have the ability to understand problems, who know where to look for solutions and who have the ability and the attitude to define and implement. Especially today, when the economic environment is getting increasingly complex and uncertain, we need fresh talent that has already gone through a structured learning and have an appreciation of what is relevant to industry. An MBA has to be seen as a basic foundation that familiarizes us with contemporary thinking, empowers us to grasp issues much faster, and tackle situations and challenges to create value. However, there is a caveat. An MBA will give the students a head-start but an

MBA is not a passport to success. Multiple factors have a bearing on the growth prospects, where the quality of the MBA can make the difference.

2. **What are the prospects for a fresh MBA in the industry and more specifically in FMCG and media Industries?**

   The general industry practice is to place MBA graduates a step ahead of non-MBAs in the organizational hierarchy at the entry level. There are opportunities across almost all functions including sales, marketing, communication, human resources, supply chain and project management. The FMCG industry and the media industry by definition require people who can manage consumer and customer expectations faster and who have the ability to capture insights and anticipate trends ahead of the others. Professionals who have gone through a rigorous MBA are expected to be better organized, more structured in their thinking, aware of consumer trends and changing lifestyles, and will do well in these fields.

3. **What are the qualities you look for in an MBA when you go for recruitments?**

   When I recruit, I assess MBAs on three levels. On the first level, I try to assess candidates for their confidence, level headedness and whose values are aligned with our organizational values of integrity, honesty, courage and teamwork and who we believe will fit into our organizational culture. At the second level, I look for leadership potential, positive attitude, curiosity and enthusiasm. The third level, of course, is the candidates' knowledge of their subject area as well as of the industry trends where they are headed. The final evaluation is a combination of all these factors, though I must admit it is only a best effort assessment. We might make mistakes and that should not discourage or depress anyone if they do not get shortlisted.

4. **What specific things an MBA should do to make a sound career in industry while studying, more specifically in FMCG and media industries?**
   Management education is an interactive process. It is about developing an ability to synthesize information, analyze with incomplete information and develop the capability to look for logical or creative solutions. Students need to take charge of their own education. Many students get stuck at trying to remember specific theories and solutions, eventually start feeling the information overload and adopt an attitude of 'need to get through' the course. The MBA opportunity is not just about sitting through the lectures and receiving information, but it is about understanding the essence of the sessions and to start relating it to practical situations. The FMCG and the media industries are constantly evolving and live examples are available all around us in shopping malls, in newspapers, on television, while making our purchase or consumption decisions. Serious students of management, who want to excel, must keep applying, even in their sleep, what they have learnt in the classroom sessions to the real life situations. The faculty has a wealth of information, has a bank of cases and past experiences that will continue growing, but there will never be enough time to assimilate all the knowledge. The students need to start thinking like professionals in their area of interest and keep pushing their instructors for greater insights.

5. **How an MBA should groom himself/herself for a better career path after joining industry?**

I have always believed that no matter where we are and what we are doing, we have to bring out the best that we are capable of. It is no different in the industry. Unfortunately, many of us tend to forget that interpersonal interaction, alignment with organizational objectives and the ability to work with teams is critical to success. What we do or what we project creates expectations amongst others and the ability to manage expectations then becomes a determinant for how your career will shape up. This is not merely a heuristic or gut feel. Organizations are now ensuring that functional and senior managers go through a 360 degree evaluation process where people who they work with internally and external to the organization provide their feedback and inputs. We need to keep evolving ourselves, while ensuring that we stay true to our own values.

Some traits that are helpful in career growth include:

- Willingness to understand the working of other functions apart from your own area of interest.
- Keep learning and stay abreast of technology and knowledge about your function and the industry.
- Learn to manage ambiguity.
- Be prepared for mobility across geographies.
- Demonstrate an ability to get things done.

Sometimes, if our values and the values of the organizations are not in synch, it may be best to course correct and look for an organization where you can align with the values. Career paths will move faster when it's a win situation for both the organization and the employees.

6. How is industry looking up for future, say next five years?

The rapid technological transformation all around

is changing the pace and styles of management for many. Industry is increasingly realizing that while processes are important, their people make the difference. They are looking for and grooming managers who are focused, fast and flexible and have the courage to take considered risks quite like entrepreneurs. I would say that five years is a long-term horizon now and a lot of transformation will happen during this time. However, there are some things that will not change. Need to understand consumer behavior will not change, though the techniques might become more sophisticated. The fundamental concepts will not change and organizations will continue to say 'Back to the basics'.

7. **Besides skills and knowledge, what kind of values you would look for in an MBA?**
   Ethical behavior and empathy are important for me. It must be the underlying foundation for any manager, irrespective of how they navigate their careers.
8. **How you think an MBA can contribute towards society and nation building?**
   Contributing to society and nation building is everyone's responsibility. However, MBAs perhaps have a bigger responsibility, because they are better educated, have a better understanding and perspective on the future of the industry and the economy and are better equipped to deal with emerging issues. They will soon reach positions of responsibility and will have the power to make decisions that will impact society. They need to remember their ethics and values and take decisions, or at least influence and persuade their colleagues and superiors to make decisions that are in the

larger interest of the nation. This is not always easy, but every effort will be important.

9. **What are the tips for MBA aspirants coming from relatively smaller towns and those whose medium of teaching has been Hindi?**

Success is not the preserve of those who speak English or who live in large towns and cities. What really matters in the long run is our aspiration, our dream and our ability to work hard to achieve our dream. If the medium of teaching till now has been Hindi, it just means that these students will have to work a little harder on learning English. They can join external classes and during the MBA course they should continue taking remedial sessions to improve. Management is not about knowing English but understanding the concepts and being able to relate to them. However, knowing English is necessary since, at least in today's corporations, much of the work is still done in English and to be able to interact well everyone must learn English. It can be overcome. Remember that we now live in a global economy and we could be sent to work in a country where we do not know the language. The only solution is then to learn and I have seen many friends and colleagues who have gone to work in China and are learning the Chinese language.

10. **What kind of preparation an aspirant should do for getting into a good B-school?**

B-school preparation needs to be planned. It starts a couple of years before you start the B-school. You must somewhat know what you want to do and thus you start the process of shortlisting schools.

There are three things that you must work on. (i) Relevant work experience where possible. (ii) Strong CAT score and (iii) Statement of purpose.

Let's look at all of them separately. Your work experience has to be in sync with what your career ambitions are. Ideally, most good schools require two years of quality work that demonstrates leadership, sustained results and potential for growth.

CAT or GMAT is a very integral part of your application process. A good score gives you buffer in case you do not have enough work experience. You ideally require 3 months of preparation to get a good score. The best way to prepare is to be strong on your basic and do a lot of mock tests.

Finally, statement of purpose. You need to have clarity on what you want to achieve out of B-school and how you see an MBA helping your future career plans.

11. How should an aspirant select a good B-school?

MBA is going to be a very important decision in your life. You must keep the following in mind when choosing a B-school: Prestige and ranking, post-MBA starting salary, teaching methodology, quality of student life, tuition fees and size of the program.

□

Huge Opportunities in Start-ups for MBA

1. **What prospects/opportunities you see for an MBA in today's scenario?**

Dr. Abhijit Nair
Senior Consultant (Ex.)
National Geography Channel

When one looks at the base level nothing much has changed from the earlier days in terms of opportunities and prospects for an MBA student. It is wonderful to be a management graduate now, as it was say, 10 years before. The opportunities in various segments have increased and the prospects in certain other segments have decreased. But the number of opportunities is almost similar. The burgeoning start-up population and their requirements have improved the outlook for management students and since this segment is very media savvy it has given out a feeling of better openings. The traditional sectors still hire for management trainee profiles and they require the marketers and the finance professionals as was the case earlier. The responsibilities and the roles that these companies need these students for has changed according to the times. This again, is not a vast change but there is considerable need of data analytical skills, ability to be comfortable on MS-Excel on every aspect, ease of using CRM tools or any kind of software tool that is beneficial for business improvements, and of course the age-old element of attitude that one carries towards all kinds of jobs. The expectation is to have some experts in certain areas like data analytics, financial analytics and sales functions but overall the holistic understanding of management, work, and largely corporate cultural fit is what the industry aspires for in the new graduates. Students that I know of have been recently placed in FMCG, banking, financial entities, FMCD, research firms, consultancies and almost all of them are at the level of management trainees.

2. **What are the prospects for a fresh MBA in the industry?**

Freshers are primarily considered for roles that require primary market understanding. All functions require the individual to gather a very clear perceptive of how the industry work-flow prevails, what market conditions exist and how to bring in profits. The fresh graduates are sent across the territories and made to plod so as to gather enough knowledge and outlook that would get them to stand their stead in the corporate world as they trudge along. The prospects for fresh graduates albeit not as good as the experienced ones; if their academic skills coupled with their ability to visualize and commit themselves to the theories and ideations in a practical scenario; augurs well for a good opportunity across the industry. There are segment-wise differentiations in acceptance of freshers but almost all of the industry looks for new graduates who are buoyant in spirit, with a learning attitude and an extraordinary amount of self-assurance. The students who are placed in the early among fresh postgraduates are almost always the ones who are excitable, with loads of energy, exuberance along with a great sense of inquisitiveness to learn and adapt.

3. **What are the qualities you look in an MBA when you go for recruitments?**

Energy, enthusiasm, vigor with an equal amount of rigor and an awesome attitude towards learning and development of self would carry a student a long way during recruitments. To simplify this thought, childlike cheerfulness with knowledge is vouched for in recruitments. The curiosity about all things under the sun and the hunger to climb up the ladder of success through constant change and erudition is the primary essence that carries and MBA student beyond. The ability to articulate all of these soft skills in a normal conversation coupled with some hard skills like an analytical mind, interpretation of intricate rhythms that are all around in business, and comfort with using information technology (IT) in their day-to-day life makes for a brilliant combination. There could be varied levels of competencies in all of the above that would be measured but some element of aptitude in all of these makes for a precise fit into the corporate schema of things. A student named Sudhanshu recently got placed with a large multinational consumer goods company purely because he had very good mix of all the mentioned competencies, they were not at very high levels but they were all available with certain aspects taking precedence over some others. This mix of proficiencies makes for a brilliant combination.

4. **What specific things a MBA should do to make a sound career in industry while studying?**

Severity in the academic side of things is extremely important. The first year constitutes of getting into the groove, having a disciplined approach to education and extensive reading in all areas. The ability to assimilate extreme amounts of information from all aspects of business, economy, politics, accountancy &c coupled with an insatiable appetite to integrate all this understanding for solving real-world problems and issues is what would make a massive difference in having a sound career. Involving in management of college events, seminars, discussions tied with live projects with industry, and research on specific and current aspects of the industry would create an approach that is more attuned to teamwork, analysis as well as crisis management. In the second year, the student would have to attune themselves to selective subjects and incorporation of all their first year learning into these specific subjects of interest so as to gather a broader overview of the area of expertise. Along with all these things, continuous practice and development of soft skills among peers and outsiders; networking over social media and industry conferences with industry people and subject matter experts should bode well for overall progress and reach.

5. **How an MBA should groom himself/herself for a better career path after joining industry?**

After joining the industry, the early stages are primarily oriented towards learning the nitty-gritty of regular everyday responsibilities and tackling daily situations and problems. Whilst doing these the ability to network with peers and managers within the organization as well as with the wider audience in similar industries helps to bring in value as well as improvement of net worth. The initial months and may be a year and half would sometimes feel like a lengthy, monotonous and arduous climb but the basics would assimilate into the system and the grueling tasks would make most MBAs welcome the grind as wells enjoy the process of foundation building. Some of them would get into extensive trainings that would help acculturate and absorb them into the demanding toil that is expected of them mentally as well as physically. The inadequacies of inexperience and hangover of academic life gives way to the wider knowledge of functions, completion of tasks, achievement of targets, communication of ideas and minutiae of operational teams that work towards a precise direction.

6. **How is industry looking up for future, say next five years?**

   Industry shall always look up. There shall be ups and downs based on the Chinese plunges, Dollar dips, European Union impediments, oil acting topsy-turvy and political upheavals but then the resurgence always shall come about through measures from governing bodies; economic counsels; financial reforms and of course controlled changes in every factor that affects business. As is with all changes, the middle-class population would get affected by the constant disruptions but the industries shall continue to adapt, adopt as well as be catalyst of further developments, innovations and improvements. For example, cloud computing may have arrived and has distressed the way we work with our computers and phones but the traditional IT and telecom sector molded itself, accepted the change and adapted, in fact, bringing in more new-age companies that got immersed with the flow of things.

7. **Besides skills and knowledge, what kind of values you would look for in an MBA?**

   An increasing tilt toward voluntary work in social causes is extremely acceptable and mandated. The millennial generation expects a lot of free hand at work as well as a more jovial and conducive environment with less hierarchy. Their aspirations are different from the previous generations. Their career choices may not be based on a long-term survival element but may be an intention of spring boarding to something that is closer to their heart. Since this is constantly being witnessed in recruitments, companies have started to need this as a binding attitude among the current generation. Passion in a particular area, entrepreneurial strains and the ability to multi-task is seen as great value additions. A positive role-model, acceptance of constructive feedbacks, appreciating opinions of others, respect for all devoid of hierarchical and social perceptions and lastly but most importantly integrity are the primary virtues that could stand any MBA apart.

8. **How you think an MBA can contribute towards society and nation building?**

   Youth's are supposed to be socially responsible. The MBA student knows how to approach a problem. The student breaks down the problem into parts and tries to find the precise construct that created the problem in the first place. What is taught in B-schools is to get to the root of the problem through a lot of queries that brings in answers that may lead elaboration of the concern at hand and clarity in approaching the issue. The primary view may be opaque but as the layers are peeled of when viewed from varied angles and birds eye visions the bigger picture emerges which in turn help to attain pin-point accuracy towards a workable solution. Society demands inclusiveness and a commitment towards betterment of all its institutions that overrides all differences. Nation building is higher subset of the same aspiration. B-schools are not only supposed to pave way for money-makers and problem solvers; both very intrinsic to social development but they are also supposed to induce social commitment among its students as a component that demands attention as well as the necessary deference. If such behavior is stimulated and fostered on a regular basis the MBA student shall be a very important cog in the wheel of social improvement and nation building. They can create a very powerful and positive impact of building the blocks of development that would act in harmony with the work done by agencies and government bodies.

9. **What are the tips for MBA aspirants coming from relatively smaller towns and those whose medium of teaching has been Hindi?**

Approximately, 422 million people speak Hindi in India, according to figures from the 2001 Census data. Now, these numbers would be close to 550 or 600 million. Medium of language at home and in the day-to-day social experiences are in Hindi. Media speaks a mix of both English and Hindi. When it comes to the working population, most sectors of country – financial, consumer goods or durables, retail, service and much more are dependent on a crowd that understands English, can converse and write a bit but can manage Hindi extremely well. The consultancies, the foreign banks, IT multinationals, the KPOs and BPOs expect extreme proficiency in the English language. All corporate that function in the South and East of India need a population that can be fluent in English because of number of regional languages that are employed in that area. Their inability in using Hindi also helps the cause of English in these territories. So if specifically considered in terms of knowledge of English among Hindi-medium MBA aspirants coming from smaller towns or villages from the Hindi belt there is a lot of strenuous activities that happen in almost all B-schools to get their level of English language improved. Although a very difficult task, aspiration-wise the student is up to the task as there is an enormous perception of the English language as the medium that shall bring success. This perception in turn helps in the student working hard, trying to speak, write, read and learn the language at a pace which may be surprising. With the exponential growth of Internet and reach of this brilliant engine of change, students from smaller towns need to watch a lot of videos, documentaries, movies, read a lot of news articles, general commentaries and also listen to a lot of podcasts, audio-books and more such wonderful innovations that are spread across the world wide web. A recent example is of student from a village further from Bhatinda in Punjab who did not have much proficiency in writing or speaking in English. As of now his writing skills have improved with the help of websites like www.hemingwayapp.com and software like Ginger. For better comprehension he is constantly watching movies and documentaries that have subtitles and this is also helping him in speech. It takes time, but the effort pays if the aspiration and direction is right.

10. **What kind of preparation an aspirant should do for getting into a good B-school?**

The first stage is the aptitude test and this primarily requires practice. Constant, every day practice that could get the student into the top 90 percentile which would make a massive difference in the kind of B-school the aspirant goes into. The ability to communicate succinctly and with confidence about all things that matter is an essential skill during group discussions and interviews. Knowledge of subject matter that was explored during graduation would better the chances of selection. General knowledge is an important category that needs regular updating. Clarity on career aspirations, enthusiasm and high spirits could make the task extremely easy.

11. How should an aspirant select a good B-school?

A good B-school is the one that creates an individual who is of sound mind and body with an extremely endearing demeanor with respect towards all people without differentiators, having exceptional communication skills, analytical abilities, brilliant understanding of business, outstanding problem solving skills, and a great motivator who can work with all kinds of teams and create synergies at places where it does not exist. Students should talk to every entity – inside and outside of all the B-schools that they feel are like the above and get a completely clear visualization of alignment with their expectations. For example, I have found that some aspirants and their parents talk to security guards, small vendors that thrive outside of B-Schools, and even the drivers of auto-rickshaws and taxis that ply in that area. It makes a lot of sense because these people are involved with the students and the community as a whole.

□

All Three Wings of Indian Defence need MBAs

1. **What prospects/opportunities you see for an MBA in today's scenario?**

Prof. (Col.) A.K. Rajpal
Former Director,
Military Training-14,
Army Headquarters,
Sena Bhavan,
New Delhi

Rise of the information society and the knowledge Economy at a global level has reinforced the role of MBAs as the key economic and business drivers. While the number of traditional employment opportunities may or may not remain to be static, entrepreneurship in the form of 'Start Ups' and other innovative techniques will drive the business graduates to make their own mark in future. Design, creativity, innovation, in the form of self-employment, aided and abetted by technology and digitization, will continue to motivate them to open up many more vistas for themselves, thereby, creating employment opportunities, as also contributing to the economy of their nation. The recently inaugurated 'Start-up Venture' by the Hon'ble Prime Minister in Vigyan

Bhavan, where one lakh fifty thousand aspirants showed up instead of its capacity of only a few thousands (as stated by the Finance Minister) is too obvious an example to be quoted in this context.

2. **What are the prospects for a fresh MBA in Army, Air force, Navy, Defense industry and other industry sectors?**

   Having been the Director of manpower planning, training, and administration in one of the Military Training Directorates at Army Headquarters, Sena Bhavan, New Delhi, I can personally vouch for a definite requirement of MBA graduates in all the three Services. While the MBAs with their management skills may be welcome in any of the Arms/Services of Army, Navy, and Air Force for the reasons of strategizing and tactful planning of any operation, and deftness in organizational development efforts, they are the crying need of the hour in ordinance. Supplies, education, medical (for hospital administration etc.), signals corps (for digitization and technology facilitation) of all the three Services. Apart from their expertise in IT (for those majoring in IT and informatics), their in-depth knowledge of 'Supply Chain', 'Human Resource Planning', 'Purchase/Acquisition Procedures' and 'Statistical Skills' will be highly conducive to better day-to-day functioning within their respective Arms and Services.

   The other Defense sectors that may welcome MBAs with open arms, in my opinion, are the Defense Research and Development Organization (DRDO) and Central Defense Accounts Services (CDA), both at Pune and in regional HQs.

3. **What are the qualities you look in an MBA when you go for recruitments?**

As evolution is the law of nature, jobs and their scope have also undergone a lot of change. When I go for recruitment, I would like to gather as much information as I can and ascertain his/her suitability for the portfolio in question. The days of mere subject knowledge and communication skills are a passé these days.

What I would look for in prospective MBA candidate is: whether his/her face is reflecting the inner mind glow; the movements and postures are active, positive, and alive; body language reflects confidence, openness, readiness and cooperation; eyes are radiating sincerity, friendliness and positive ideas; voice shows warmth and depth of knowledge; and whether he/she is a problem solver or problem creator.

4. **What specific things an MBA should do to make a sound career in industry while studying?**

The more educated and productive they are, the more soundness in industry they will display. Choosing the right path for their brighter future will depend upon what they love and are passionate about.

Having said that, a true global exposure with peer-to-peer learning with students from different countries for developing an in-depth understanding of cultural diversity; research-oriented approach towards all the curriculum subjects; a keen desire to acquire more and more industry centric certifications while studying; and intensive practices in high end technology labs with advanced computing facilities within their institutions are a few areas for concentration for and by the MBAs to develop the job security, if they are looking for a sustained career in the industry. Herein, the institutions will also have to supplement lecture-based pedagogy by simulations, cases, live projects, and outbound trainings.

5. **How an MBA should groom himself/herself for a better career path after joining industry?**
"An individual is solely responsible for his/her growth during the entire career span," so say the sages in the corporate world. Nevertheless, I am of the firm opinion that the industry/organizations cannot shy away from grooming the employees, once they are firmly on board. Organizations can assist the intellectual and behavioral growth needs by providing on-line tools and portals, which have learning-oriented modules on the areas of operations; encourage dialogue between the CEO, senior leadership and the employees on work dynamics; and not create unreasonable expectations by making them more interesting and exciting than the job itself.
My premise to base this argument is that smart people (and MBAs are smart) are not the ones who are averse to learning. They are enthusiastic. Organizations just need to understand and introduce training initiatives that would entice them to learn more each day.
6. **How are defense/industry looking up for future MBAs, say next five years?**
Be it Defense or industry, leadership is important in every sphere of life. Wealth generators of tomorrow can actually be 'Value Generators'. There could be, in my opinion, seven step codes for success for the emerging leaders of tomorrow in both the sectors. WSSP HTC, an acronym for Work Habits, Sensitivity, Skills and Knowledge, Proactive Approach, Hunger for Exploration, Team Work, and Communication Skills.
7. **Besides skills and knowledge, what kind of values you would look for in an MBA?**

I would like to list them as, belief in one self; getting out of comfort zone; being around the best; setting realistic goals; maintaining interpersonal relationships (IPR); avoid seeing crises or stressful events as unbearable problems; accepting circumstances that cannot be changed; keeping a long term perspective; visualizing what is wished; and taking care of mind, body and personal needs and feelings.

8. **How you think an MBA can contribute towards society and nation building?**

   MBAs will always have an edge over others for contribution towards society and nation building. Management is central to every sector and discipline in nation building. To confine their contribution to a particular area or arena will be an injustice to them. From tackling unemployment by way of initiating Start-Ups to participation in public affairs of economic and social growth to undertaking the management of uncertain environment of health care to volunteering for urbanization and rural development to indulgence in innovations for manufacturing, export orientations, environment conservation, and infrastructure construction to inculcating the sense of community and camaraderie through team work to, finally, deft management of finances, MBAs have been and will continue to build societies and nation to greater heights.

9. **What are the tips for MBA aspirants coming from relatively smaller towns and those whose medium of teaching has been Hindi?**

   Yes, this imbalance needs to be treated with all earnestness, as the MBA aspirants from the rural stock is increasing by the day. There may have to be a two-pronged approach: Firstly, efforts on the part

of candidates themselves. They have to maintain or enhance self esteem, listen and respond with a sense of deep involvement in classroom curriculum, seek help and support freely, share thoughts and feelings with respective guides, mentors, and teachers. On the other side, the institutions so located have to ensure that they do not rush to fix the problems and be individualistic in approach, do away with one-size-fits-all philosophy, shun avoiding tough issues, stop inconsistent application across different contexts, and never neglect to coach in the moment.
□

Middle Level Positions have MBA Requirements in Engineering

1. **What prospects/opportunities you see for an MBA in today's scenario?**
   MBA is always important for shaping your career. Even in today's scenario, whether anyone looks forward to strengthening their career in the area of entrepreneurship or have their goal well focused on escalating the corporate rung, it is important to have a MBA degree. The corporate look for an MBA as they have an insight into the tricks &acumen necessary for competent handling of business and segments constituting it.

Mr. Neeraj Sharan
Chief Operating Officer
Greaves Cotton Ltd.

2. **What are the prospects for a fresh MBA in industry and organizations like Greaves?**
   Greaves is not different than any other corporate that also look for these specific skill set. Being an Engineering company we look for more of fresh Engineer Graduate than MBA. We prefer MBA for middle level positions and hence look for few years of experience for induction.
3. **What are the qualities you look in an MBA when**

you go for recruitments?

Every MBA students brings something unique to the table, but we are always on the lookout for specific qualities such as – Leadership Quality, display quantitative competency, set realistic long term and short term goal for himself/herself and adopt to changing environment.

4. **What specific things an MBA should do to make a sound career in industry while studying?**

   MBA teaches many things to shape your future but according to me the two most important things a MBA graduate should focus is statistics and accounting. Any business manager needs to know how to budget and how to read a financial statement. And in statistics, you learn to use the science of probability to forecast the future. This skill is crucial for people involved in strategy and in planning the future of an organization. The case studies taught in the MBA classes should be more from the current practical situation of the companies in the current scenario.

5. **How an MBA should groom himself/herself for a better career path after joining industry?**

   MBA Students study the concepts of management in their classes but hardly understand how this knowledge can be applied in real business scenario; there is thus a gap in application. As students, it is imperative to understand what business is all about and how you can contribute to the growth of any organisation.

6. **How is Engineering, Manufacturing and other industry looking up for future, say next 5 years?**

   The Engineering and Manufacturing is going into bad phase. The slow economic recovery continues to hinder expansion and growth opportunities, recent government and industry reports show an uptick in capital investment funding. Manufacturers are becoming more focused on capturing value through innovation and speed to market.

7. **Besides Skills and knowledge, what kind of values you would look for in an MBA?**
   Beside Skill and Knowledge the Value which matters for an MBA who is going to be a Leader is a good human being, disciplined, Focused and versatile.
8. **How You think an MBA can contribute towards society and nation building?**
   MBAs can create an impact on the society as they have resources and avenues. A body of skilled people in any society has a powerful positive impact on development of that society. They have the responsibility to use their skill, talent and capability to create an impact on the societal and environmental issues being faced by the Nation. It's their responsibility to move away from just looking at profits towards creating a business which is more socially responsible and inclusive.
9. **What are the tips for MBA aspirants coming from relatively smaller towns and those whose medium of teaching has been Hindi?**
   Communication skills, undoubtedly, play a real important and crucial role in professional life in corporate India. Focus on polishing communication skills in English.
   Keep updating and refreshing your knowledge through peer learning. Participate in all kinds of group activities like group case studies, simulations, industry interaction programmes and inter- college level academic and extra-curricular competitions. Technical knowledge along with good inter personal skills are the key qualities companies look for in a potential candidate. Focus on improving these skills right from the commencement of the course.

□

Assured Opportunities in Oil Energy and Petroleum Sectors

1. **What prospects/opportunities you see for an MBA in today's scenario?**

Prof. M.S. Kumar
Head (Retd.),
Panipat Refinery,
Indian Oil Corporation

Prospects and Opportunities for an MBA in today's scenario:

- MBA grads have distinct advantage of being a Generalist Business Manager rather than being a specialist technocrat. This provides them the cutting edge in industry.
- In today's scenario, business opportunities are emerging in all sectors across the globe. MBA graduates can identify new business opportunities with greater ease both in local and global markets.
- MBA graduates acquire skills in networking and collaboration in a virtual organization, which help them manage complex supply chains in the industry.
- Networking and collaboration skills provide tremendous business opportunities in service sector specially for entrepreneurs

- MBA graduates can handle stress better than others and can also encounter failures with determination to succeed

2. **Prospects for fresh MBA in oil/energy/ infrastructure sectors.**

   Oil sector provides extensive business opportunities in Sourcing and Logistics services in Oil movement and Storage facilities (OM&S).

   Oil sector also throws open unlimited business opportunities in marketing and distribution of petroleum products as well as safe and timely delivery of those products in all forms namely solid, liquid and gas to end consumers across all geographical regions both within the country as well as across the globe.

   Natural gas reserves both in India and outside, especially from gas surplus nations such as Iran, provide ample opportunity in transportation of gas through cross country pipelines and marketing of a host of gas-based products such as fertilizers and petrochemicals products.

   With decline of reserves for fossil fuel, need for developing alternate energy sources is assuming greater importance. India has tremendous potential for harnessing solar power & wind power. MBA grads can deploy available technology and avail entrepreneurial opportunities in this sector.

   Infrastructure sector provides exponential growth for MBA graduates, especially in the areas of construction projects, bullet trains and smart cities projects, etc.

   'Make in India' and 'Digital India' initiatives of the government are bound to snow ball into new opportunities for budding managers from B-schools

3. **Qualities one would like to see in MBA grads during placement interviews.**

Knowledge:

General awareness about the macro & micro environment

Comprehensive knowledge about the industry

Knowledge about the particular company opted for recruitment.

Vision and mission/business model/business processes/supply chain/competitive strengths and weakness in the industry

Academic knowledge related to the particular function

Attitude & Skills:

Ability to work in teams and 'Get along with People' at all levels

Ability to plan and organize

Exercise flexibility and ability to cope with stress at the workplace

Ability to sell Ideas or products

Creative and innovative thinking skills.

4. **What specific things an MBA should do to make a sound career in industry while studying?**

Models/flow diagram/metrics in text books provide comprehensive and logical thinking skills. They can be easily stored in hard disc of the brain. Students in MBA should pay attention to learning of such models and process diagrams and develop skills in relating to them in logical sequence while answering questions in the exams or interviews and also for making presentations in corporate career. They help provide a framework for asking as well as giving SMART answers.

I have derived benefit from this approach during my own academic as well as professional career in Indian Oil.

In exams for MBA students I always insist for explaining the concept with the help of diagrams taught in the class.

Further, I believe selling skills are best learnt by making presentations during academic courses. I would strongly recommend MBA students to seek opportunities for making presentations on different topics in class as well as in other events in the campus.

5. **How an MBA should groom himself/herself for a better career path after joining industry?**

In a good organization, career path for every manager is prepared in advance by the HR head in consultation with the respective functional head and the concerned individual.

I had the privilege of working in different functions in IOC under the job rotation scheme in pursuance of the pre-designed career path set for my growth and development. I started my professional career as Assistant Electrical Engineer responsible for Operations and Maintenance of Power Plant. By virtue of job rotation at different levels of hierarchy, I acquired knowledge and experience of working in process re-engineering, materials planning, procurement & inventory control, HRD & training functions, quality, health, safety & environment mgmt. Construction of refinery projects and general management of SBU.

In my opinion MBA grads should seek job rotations for career advancement within the company. If the company provides a well-designed career path, the manager should readily accept the same and treat the change as an opportunity for growth. In case the organization does not provide job rotation as a policy, one should request for the same during annual appraisal interviews. However, it is important to identify desired skill set for career growth in the chosen functional area and plan to acquire them gradually either by rotations within or by hopping outside the organization.

I also strongly recommend for fresh MBAs to show case their contribution in non-routine areas along with their achievements in routine areas during appraisal interviews.

Such contributions can be made at the workplace by using 3-M techniques (MURI, MURA and MUDA). Identify some process or activities that are unnecessary (MURI). Eliminate such activities or re-engineer the process to improve productivity. Similarly, identify bottleneck (MURA) in any process of work and remove them to augment productivity. Lastly identify wastes (MUDA) at the workplace and reduce or eliminate the waste to improve quality and productivity.

Creative contribution of MBAs in any of the aforesaid areas goes a long way to earn feather in the cap for the fresher and helps create a personal brand image in the organization. During my teaching MBA students I constantly remind them about this approach and inspire them to set personal goals for such achievements.

6. **How is industry looking up for future, say next 5 years?**

Ours being a growing economy, future for fresh MBAs appears to be sufficiently bright for the next five years.

Initiatives of the new government shall fructify within 4-5 years, which will help usher into plethora of business opportunities in India.

Rural sector is poised for inclusive growth due to resultant effects of infrastructural developments and Make in India thrust.

Both manufacturing as well as the service sector will grow at a fast speed, however, service sector is likely to grow faster.

Tremendous opportunities lie ahead in agri business, food processing, capacity building in world class storage and warehousing facilities, modernization of logistics and ITES. Aggregation strategy in major areas of supply chain management, namely sourcing, warehousing, transportation and inventory mgmt. hold immense opportunities for 3-PL services providers. In this regard Uber & OLA Taxi Services are good examples of business application of aggregation strategy.

7. **Besides skills and knowledge, what kind of values you would look for in an MBA?**

Ethics and integrity are two values which I rate high and would recommend for nurturing by budding managers of tomorrow.

In my professional career in IOC, I earned respect and recognition by nurturing concern for subordinate development. During MDPs for practicing managers as well during classroom teaching in MBA, I do emphasize the need and importance of subordinate development inspire audience to nurture this activity. I believe this is one of the most effective techniques in Team Building.

8. **How you think an MBA can contribute towards society and nation building?**

- MBA graduates can contribute significantly towards workplace improvements with the help of the team members. Organizations stand to acquire sustainable growth due to the sigma effect of such small contributions. Needless to mention, growth and development of individual organizations eventually snow ball into economic growth at the macro level which in turn contributes towards nation building.

I often emphasize and recommend following five managerial practices for my students in MBA as well as for line managers in industry for making Workplace improvements.

Contribute to improvements in quality and Productivity through application of MURI, MURA and MUDA.

Practice Deming's PDCA Cycle for systematic execution of work.

Avoid rework by doing it right first time and every time.

Invest your gold to generate five bronze medalist in your team.

Never accept single solution to any problem of the workplace rather encourage the team to produce 4-5 creative solutions.

9. What are the tips for MBA aspirants coming from relatively smaller towns and those whose medium of teaching has been Hindi?

Though English is widely used language in management studies and in business communication across the globe, proficiency in other official language, such as Hindi does not create barrier in business interactions or in doing business at global level. Services of interpreters can always be hired for translating talks in any language into English and vice versa.

China is a burning example where GDP touched double digits in growth rate despite their proficiency in English being poorer.

Business interactions only require clarity in thoughts and in expressions. Managers, who have been brought up in small towns and have received education up to graduation level in Hindi, need not consider themselves handicapped. However, it is a good idea to pursue English-speaking class to acquire some fluency in English.

Think and crystallize ideas and thoughts in Hindi and participate in discussions without any inhibition.

□

Entrepreneurship is on the Rise Under 'Made in India' Campaign

1. **What prospects/opportunities you see for an MBA in today's scenario?**

Dr. Sanjay Pande
Assistant Registrar
I.I.T. Delhi

The prospects and opportunities for MBA are available not only in private corporations but also in government jobs. In fact, there has been an increasing trend of MBA students opting for premier services. In fact, as per the annual report of Union Public Service Commission, about 35 candidates from IIMs qualified in the Civil Services Examinations-2012. The trend has been growing ever since.

This apart, with the growing emphasis of the Government of India on entrepreneurship by way of Make in India, Start-up India Stand up India, Unnat Bharat and numerous such initiatives, huge and exhilarating opportunities appear on the horizon for MBAs in the country.

2. **What are the prospects for a fresh MBA in the industry?**

Industry is always on a look out for fresh MBAs to spearhead its business propositions. If a candidate has necessary skills, capabilities and knowledge there is no dearth of opportunities. In fact, the opportunities abound and are varied.

3. **What are the qualities you look in an MBA when you go for recruitments?**

The first and the foremost quality a recruiter looks in an MBA is his preparedness for the job. With the growing competitiveness and complexity, the corporations would ideally look for a candidate who is ready to jump into the work straightaway. This readiness is not only in terms of theoretical concepts but in terms of appreciation of the realities of the industry and the company hiring the candidate.

The preparedness must, however, be accompanied with a "growth mindset". Meaning that the candidate is willing to learn and grow. The willingness is reflected in the initiative one shows and hard work one is prepared to undertake.

The third quality a recruiter look for is the attitude of a solution provider. The world is replete with people who point out towards deficiencies and problems. But corporate world requires people who can suggest solutions to the problems and then take responsibility to implement that solution.

4. **What specific things an MBA should do to make a sound career in industry while studying?**

The first and the foremost thing an MBA should do is to develop a general appreciation of the business. The MBA education today creates managers who are experts at one of the many silos – HR/finance/marketing/sales, etc. But none of them, individually, is business. To develop a sound career in industry, it is very essential that an MBA has a theoretical as well as practical appreciation of the entire structure. To ensure this, one needs to not only take up courses seriously but attempt to expose oneself to industry practices by way of short-term projects, internships, industry visits, general interaction with the corporates, attending seminars, conferences, case studies, etc.

This apart, MBA is the best time to fill the gaps. There are students who lack in skills (e.g. oral, verbal, etc.), There are other students who lack in knowledge, (E.g. I was always afraid of finance). Then there are students who have behavioural issues (too shy, too introvert, lacking confidence). The MBA time is the time to take on to these challenges head on. One can approach the teachers to handle these issues or look around for exemplars in the B-school in the area of their concern and try to find out the reason for their excellence. Alternatively, one can seek the help from alumni in the specific area of concern. The possibilities are infinite. You just got to get willing to emerge a new and powerful individual once you are over with your MBA.

5. **How an MBA should groom himself/herself for a better career path after joining industry?**

   Learning is an ongoing process. There is no definitive answer to this question for it depends on your needs. You may have a need to upgrade your skills, capabilities of knowledge and that is what you have to do upgrade them.

   Nonetheless, one essential thing one needs to do after joining the industry is, become a master of your industry. One must not only become aware of the organisational structure, hierarchies, business, products, services, competitors, strengths, opportunities, and weaknesses of one's company but also develop an understanding of real value created by one's company. Yet the process should not end with an appreciation of one's company or industry. The process must ceaselessly continue to develop an appreciation of the economy, society, legal structure of the country and world at large. Why? Well that's because, these are times of growing complexity and connectedness. One's strength in these times is ones awareness. The higher is one's awareness, the more likelihood is one's chances of success. For example, we always find an employee in the company who seem to be having solutions to all the problems in the company. One might wonder how he can be so resourceful. But it is easy. He is resourceful because he has heightened awareness. Where others have a limited vision on a given problem, he can look at the problem from various angles and arrive at a solution. Therefore, it is essential that once one joins the industry, one keeps working relentlessly to expand one's awareness. That not only helps add value to the company but to the individual, thereby opening many doors of opportunities in future.

6. **How is industry looking up for future, say next five years?**

This doesn't matter. There has been no time in the economic history of earth when the industry was not looking for a skilful, knowledgeable, talented, hardworking and resourceful employee. In fact at the times of economic distress, the industries appetite for such employees increase manifold. Imagine, the time of economic depression, industries closing down, inflation rising and buyers not willing to shell out money. If there is a star salesman for luxury hotels, who has the reputation of cracking the toughest deals in the industry, what are the chances of companies cutting throat to have that employee on its rolls?

7. **Besides skills and knowledge, what kind of values you would look for in an MBA?**

   Honesty. And this is not some general, global answer.

   In fact, honesty tells a lot. As a recruiter, behind every answer one gives to my question in interview or even after I engage someone on job, if an employee is honest, I will like to retain him. Because if one is honest with others, will be honest with one. Honesty, emerges from courage. And this is not some superficial courage. To remain honest one needs to be courageous to handle not only worldly challenges but also the challenges of within. So someone is honest, it reflects one's inherent courage. If one has courage, there is always a chance to improve, grow and excel.

   This apart an honest person inspires trust. The trust, in turn, is the essence of powerful human relations. Who would like to lose out on a trust resource? No one.

8. **How you think an MBA can contribute towards society and nation building?**

   Any person doing his job religiously and honestly is contributing towards society and nation building.

   An MBA, however, due to the very nature of his training and the system as obtained in our country is much more suitably placed than those from other education streams to take up entrepreneurship or civil services and/or non profit organisations. In fact, there are numerous examples of MBAs joining politics and doing exceedingly well. Shri P. Chidamabarm, ex-Finance Minister, and Shri Jayant Sinha, present Minister of State for Finance are both MBAs.

9. **What are the tips for MBA aspirants coming from relatively smaller towns and those whose medium of teaching has been Hindi?**

Be proud of your past but increase your awareness of the world.

If your medium of instruction has been Hindi and you have difficulty in communicating in English, you need to work on it. But remember, learning English is not a must for effective communication. In fact, I have come across some people who speak so good Hindi that you would never ever notice their lack of English skills.

English is required today because an unfathomed source of knowledge and information today is available in English. Some of the best books on managements, some of the best AV resources on management are available only in English. Case studies designed in best of the B-schools are available in English. Some essential newspapers, magazines, journals are only in English. Online courses of Ivy League Schools are all in English.

Therefore, it is not that without English you will not be accepted in elite business circle or that you will be considered and outcaste in English-speaking business club, that I suggest getting a grip over English but because, you will be devoid of world's best knowledge and information repository if you are not fluent in English, that I strongly recommend to get a grip over English. So approach the issue not with a feeling that you are culturally backward but with a feeling of thirst for greater awareness of world.

As you do that, be fearless and be willing to make mistakes. No English will be learnt if you do not speak it. Speak up. Speak up at every chance. At first you will make people laugh but that is ok. That is a price you are paying for something you don't know. Soon – as you learn the language – these smiles will die out and will be replaced with an expression of amazement on the faces of onlookers.

10. **What kind of preparation an aspirant should do for getting into a good B-school? How should an aspirant select a good B-school?**

A good B-school is the one who can help you fill your gaps in skills, knowledge and capabilities and then provide you opportunities to grow as an individual. Placements are essential but a good candidate in any B-school will always get job opportunity. Further, if you are looking for some credible source of information on performance a B-school, Ministry of MHRD has come up with a transparent and very scientific National Institutional Ranking Framework based on comprehensive parameters. Have a look at it.

□

Opportunities Galore in Health Sector

1. **What prospects/opportunities you see for an MBA in today's scenario?**

   In the backdrop of the Chinese economy witnessing a downturn, India is poised to be amongst the very few economies posting a YoY GDP growth. The thrust towards Make in India, relaxation of FDI in sectors such as Defence and the recent push and relaxation towards Start-ups are going to propel the economy and open up a multitude of opportunities for MBA pass-outs like never before. The recent investment by Soft Bank, KKR, Carlyle amongst several other private enterprises is a testimony to the opportunities awaiting to get unfolded.

Mr. Yateesh Wahal
Director
Nayati Health Care and Research

2. **What are the prospects for a fresh MBA?**

   In the industry especially in health industry health and education are largely sectors which have predominantly remained unscathed from the economic cycle. Healthcare typically is a capital intensive sector and accordingly its benefits haven't percolated down to the lowest strata. This has called for a disruptive approach wherein models have been evolved to reduce the cost of delivering healthcare through innovative delivery models. Focus on primary and preventive healthcare is another promising area gaining pace with several international players including NHS acclaimed institutions piloting the concept of speciality clinics providing OPD and diagnostics facilities in a setting away from the typical disease burden of a hospital. The sector is also witnessing exposure from several non-medical corporate. HCL Avitas is once such concept which has gained momentum. The Kirloskars have also ventured into healthcare with Sakara in Bangaluru. Accordingly, the need for professional hospital managers and analytics is gaining pace and is also resulting in specialised programmes to hone the skillsets of people attempting to make a career in healthcare. Allied industries such as pharma, medical equipment manufacturing amongst others are also registering double digit growth and would be much sought after.

3. **What are the qualities you look in an MBA when you go for recruitments?**

   As the saying goes, common sense is the most uncommon quality available in the present time. The real-day conflicts do not figure in classroom discussions nor do they come up with any readymade concoctions. Solutions require presence of mind and logical reasoning and thought process which are qualities an interviewer attempts to identify in a potential candidate within the short interaction available. A candidate therefore must therefore attempt to catch the attention of the interviewer and should be in a position to drive home the point with reasoning. In essence, communication is essential.

4. **What specific things an MBA should do to make a sound career in industry while studying?**
   If a candidate is clear about the industry once aspires to join, he/she should attempt to assimilate insights and understanding about the sector and showcase the commitment level and seriousness. This would set the person apart and help make the cut while appearing for a prospective opening.
5. **How an MBA should groom himself/herself for a better career path after joining industry?**
   One should always be open to learning and suggestions for it's never too late in life to pick up something new.
6. **How is industry looking up for future, say next five years?**
   India is poised to grow over the next decade and we have an exciting canvas ahead with ample space for each one of us to paint a masterpiece.
7. **Besides skills and knowledge, what kind of values you would look for in an MBA?**
   Trust your skills and knowledge and never let go of your integrity.
8. **How you think an MBA can contribute towards society and nation building?**
   Even the smallest effort matters. One successful entrepreneur and enterprise provides employment to numerous direct and indirect setups and thus contributes to the economy and nation building. Every step and effort therefore counts.
9. **What are the tips for MBA aspirants coming from relatively smaller towns and those whose medium of teaching has been Hindi?**
   There is no substitute to hard work. For those from relatively smaller towns, put in a few extra hours and make it a point to go through one prominent

national and business daily as a matter of routine without any lag of any form.

10. What kind of preparation an aspirant should do for getting into a good B-school?

Put you heart in pursuing a sector you enjoy and visualise yourself in. The process would become that much easier however there is no substitute to hard work.

11. How should an aspirant select a good B-school?

Faculty, infrastructure, alumni are the basic pillars bearing testimony about the institution and should be researched while exercising choice.

☐

Indian Retail Sectors is World's Fifth largest and Throws Huge Potential

1. **What prospects/opportunities you see for an MBA in today's scenario?**

   Mr. Gorav Tripathi
   Deputy Manager
   Pantaloons, Gurgaon

   In year 2009 when I came out of Jaipuria campus, I did not have much preference to pick up the industry or company where I could see my career growing, however in today's scenario with maturing retail industry and 100s of starts up I believe todays MBA have a plethora of options available to choose from. In fact with the current government programs as Startup India, option of starting up one's own set up is open.

2. **What are the prospects for a fresh MBA in the industry especially in retail industry and organization like Pantaloons?**

   Retail is growing at a very fast pace in India. With retailers like H&M and ZARA, the market has become competitive not only in terms of capturing the market with maximum sales numbers but also to hire the best of the talent. In such a scenario, it's a great situation for any MBA graduate, wherein he has choice of comparing the best pay package and a comfortable environment where he wants to work and grow. As far as Pantaloons is concerned, it's a growing business, post the recent acquisition from Future Group now it's one of the youngest and biggest fashion retail business of Aditya Birla Group. The organization plans to mark its presence in almost all the tier two and three cities post a splendid expansion in metros, and such level of expansion won't be possible without the right human capital. For any fresh MBA graduate Pantaloons has a well-defined Management Trainee program which helps any MBA to choose and grow in verticals like HR, Marketing, Visual Merchandizing and Retail Operations.

3. **What are the qualities you look in an MBA when you go for recruitments?**

   To start with anything, one should have right attitude. Retail is a demanding industry which asks you to work on weekends and festivals, also the working hours are long at times. The first thing we look into any candidate is her/his ability to learn new things and willingness to accept the retail culture. The candidate should possess good communication skills, basic hold on numbers and mobility in terms of location.

4. **What specific things an MBA should do to make a sound career in industry while studying?**

   I believe one should start to identify his area of interest in terms of function and industry during the first year of MBA program post a thorough research and with the help of faculty, and accordingly should plan his internship. We see many MBA students leaving their job in the first six months of placement, that's mainly because of expectation mismatch. So the first advice is to choose what you really want to pursue as career and don't run after jobs, few basic skills which really helps any candidate to be absorbed in any retail industry are good communication skills , command over basic mathematics (comfort with business terms and numbers), good domain knowledge and command over MS Office , specially MS Excel.

5. **How an MBA should groom himself/herself for a better career path after joining industry?**
   It's important to work on the foundation post you join the industry, it takes time to learn and understand any new industry/job. One should not be impatient just after few months, one should spend time to understand the essentials of the job, perform the assigned tasks in the utmost effective manner. In particular retail industry where every inch of the space is counted, what matters is how much business you generate and your ability to make necessary corrections in case something is not working out. To grow in retail one must have excellent understating of basic retail operations, business and ways to increase profitability. The most important is flexibility to adapt to a new location and business market.

6. **How is industry looking up for future, say next five years?**
   Retailing in India is one of the strongest pillars of its economy and accounts for about 22 percent of its GDP. The Indian retail market is estimated to be US$ 500 billion and one of the top five retail markets in the world by economic value. India is one of the fastest growing retail markets in the world, with 1.2 billion people. Post the FDI reform in India,

it will certainly grow and with the new entrants in the market tremendous growth is expected. With e-commerce getting stronger day by day India might experience a new type of retail which could possibly be combination of brick and mortar and e-commerce as Omni channel.

7. **Besides skills and knowledge, what kind of values you would look for in an MBA?**

   At Aditya Birla group we have five integral values (integrity, commitment, passion, speed and Seamlessness) which are deep rooted in all the ABG Businesses. I believe in today's lucrative world wherein you have so many shortcuts to make money, we definitely look for someone with highest level of integrity.

8. **How you think an MBA can contribute towards society and nation building?**

   Well in today's time I believe that only by working for NGOs or government organization or Army does not mean that you have opportunity to work for society and contribute in nation building. By doing your job properly and effectively you are serving both the causes, for example if you in sales job by giving the right product to the customer without intentions to cheat and make the customer happy is your contribution towards building a happier and good society. As an HR we contribute by hiring people from different part of society and give them chance to make retail careers as an option and become employable. Be honest to your profession I guess that's one way of your contribution.

9. **What are the tips for MBA aspirants coming from relatively smaller towns and those whose medium of teaching has been Hindi.**

   This question is my favorite as I relate myself with

this question, I come from a city called Gorakhpur and completed my primary and secondary education through Hindi medium. Trust me it's difficult to learn English when you have never seen English as a language. My suggestion to all such MBA aspirants is that, we know English as subject and are excellent at grammar, start looking English as a language and not as a difficult subject to pass the exam, start thinking in English rather than translating and then speaking, read English newspapers and try and get into a good English language institute which can teach you basics of it and give you a good atmosphere to practice if you don't have such environment at home.

10. **What kind of preparation an aspirant should do for getting into a good B-school?**

As an MBA aspirant all of us aim for the IIMs. Aiming high is not bad, however one should know one's strength. Start from early days of graduation if you are firm to achieve the best. Take mock tests to assess your preparations and accordingly make list of colleges which you are targeting to get in.

11. **How should an aspirant select a good B-school?**

One should not only look at the placement records of the campus, you should check the alumnus list of the campus and their achievements. Most of the campus boast of their 100 percent placements, but it's the knowledge imparted by the faculties that prepares students to survive in the cruel competitive world. So look for the experiences of the faculties, success stories of the alumnus and companies who have been frequently visiting the campus.

□

Travel, Tourism and Hospitality are Strong Emerging Faces in India

1. **What prospects/opportunities you see for an MBA in today's scenario?**

   Mr. Divyam Johri
   Senior Sales Manager
   The Oberoi Group

   The past year has seen tremendous growth of development projects into India and strong promotion of 'Make in India' campaign is making inroads with global corporations to continue not only their service management programs with Indian talent but also move blue collar platform under manufacturing in various sectors opened for private equity investments. This is leading to a very healthy pace for opportunities with services and infrastructure development companies. MBAs today are gearing up to manage the increase demand and complete the industry gap which was existing before with trained talents.

2. **What are the prospects for a fresh MBA in the industry especially in Hospitality industry and organizations like The Oberoi Group?**

   Travel & Tourism Hospitality is the front face for the entire economy and is dependent on the same to forecast trends such as increase in commercial demand with FDI and consortiums entering into India need to organize stay management as well as showcase for their products and services on offer through MICE and conference events. Leisure travel becomes cyclic to the world economy with positive sentiments of trade more payouts-bonus happen globally and India provides a suitable and sustainable platform to spend on holidays.

MBAs are required in various segments under hospitality sector for Sales-Marketing engagements along with Finance and Supply chain management.

3. **What are the qualities you look in an MBA when you go for recruitments?**

   Some of the key selection points would be to assess candidates on the following parameters:

   - Communique: excellent command over fluency and written English and foreign language is a preferred advantage.
   - Analytical proficiency skill must include Microsoft Excel and Power Point along with various other business programs of learning.
   - Candidate must be well read with local/regional/national and international affairs and trends across industries as we cater to global guests who are travelling for various engagements and being well versant in the same would help in assessment of situations and guest requirements. Candidates with prior work experience in relevant industry or experience as such are more than likely to have much better success rate in any job interviews as they can answer and showcase abilities for management skills as required against any fresher.

4. **What specific things an MBA should do to make a sound career in industry while studying?**

Hospitality sector is very demanding and ability to multi-task and engagement with optimum skill sets are essential. It is recommended to be observant and learn the basics of CRM in order to ensure experiential service and life time engagement with customers.

5. **How an MBA should groom himself/herself for a better career path after joining industry?**
   Keep connecting with more and more engagements with consumers and international buyers from across the world will keep you relevant and in demand over competition. It is important to be observant and responsive to market conditions scenarios for active promotions along with insight into buying patterns of consumers.
6. **How is industry looking up for future, say next five years?**
   Positive and fast paced.
7. **Besides skills and knowledge, what kind of values you would look for in an MBA?**
   Pleasing personality along with impeccable grooming is a must in this industry, in line of our industry norms 'We are Ladies & Gentlemen serving Ladies & Gentlemen'.
8. **How you think an MBA can contribute towards society and nation building?**
   Absolutely. Corporate social responsibility projects are essential in each industry and MBA professionals can drive positive change with social projects along with contribution of man hours.
9. **What are the tips for MBA aspirants coming from relatively smaller towns and those whose medium of teaching has been Hindi?**
   Extremely essential to work on your communique – which would include fluency in English and

grooming along with skill sets you would attain during the course of study. Hindi should not be a challenge to your efforts if your overall personality is well managed and intent to learn global languages such as English with conversational fluency at least.

10. **What kind of preparation an aspirant should do for getting into a good B-school?**

    Study hard for data interpretation and logical reasoning along with work on developing your personality with grooming, current affairs.

11. **How should an aspirant select a good B-school?**

    Most candidates look at placements being the top criteria for B-school selection which is incorrect to the extent that you would still get a better job opportunity if your fundamentals and learning are correct. I recommend candidate should look at the faculty education along with number of years' experience they have in the subject along with papers, thesis and other industry relevant engagements they have had both at institutional level and individual level.

    Infrastructure and corporate engagements are also key selection points for any candidate.

    Remember, it is an investment you do to enhance your ability and skills.

□

In a Gentle Way, You can Shake the World

1. **What prospects/opportunities you see for an MBA in today's scenario?**

   Shilpi Shukla
   Senior Manager
   Hindware Limited

   MBA is not a prerequisite for entering into business. I think it gives you and edge and it's better to have firm knowledge of the recent market trends across the globe to cope up with the global competition.

   MBA students gain many skills that are easily transferable to the career choices. If students have a clear idea in which sector they would wish to pursue as a career, it would be a wise choice to consider taking up a specialized MBA course as these courses take longer to complete than a broad MBA course, however they are more marketable and appealing to a business.

   But embarking on an intensive course without some soul-searching might leave you at a disadvantage later on.

2. **What are the prospects for a fresh MBA in the industry especially in organizations like Hindware Industry?**

These days companies are investing huge effort and time in developing the pipeline for 'YL' (Young Leaders). They are fresh MBA graduates who would be on fast pedestal within the organization and would get exposed to work cross-functionally in teams and build the skills that will allow you to develop your career and progress within the company.

3. **What are the qualities you look in an MBA when you go for recruitments?**

   When you are sit for a placement you step on a treadmill which will take you through rigorous mental drills through GD, case studies, role play and assessment tests. Employers on prime facie look for the following traits in an individual:

   Intellectual ability: A candidate who is smart and mature enough to handle the stressful demands of the job. Some call it common sense.

   Quantitative orientation: A candidate who can "do" numbers.

   Analytical mindset: A candidate who is able to think critically and tolerate complex, open-ended problems.

   Team player: A candidate who works well with others and who operates smoothly and constructively in collaborative situations.

   Creativity and innovation: A candidate who is comfortable with change and ready to use it creatively.

   The killer instinct: A candidate who is not afraid of winning and seeing others lose.

4. **What specific things an MBA should do to make a sound career in industry while studying?**

   One should invest his/her time in attending guest lectures and understanding how to bridge the gap between syllabus and the practical scenario in the corporate world by doing various case studies, participating in various clubs, seminars and conferences, etc.

5. **How an MBA should groom himself/herself for a better career path after joining industry?**

   To hone the soft skills and enhance overall grooming of the MBA students, they should do a lot of mock interview involving rounds of panel interviews with senior MBA students or even classmates, should attend workshops/training sessions by leading industry experts on resume writing, interview skills, networking skills and professional code and ethics etc.

Focusing on

- How to face GD/Interview.
- Better understanding of companies' perspective (DNA Matching) – As when a company goes for a hiring, they have in mind a DNA mapping of their organization and seek for a candidate who is the best possible fit in the frame.
- Body language.
- Essentials of resume writing.

6. **How is industry looking up for future, say next five years?**

   The industry look promising with the kind of policies and reforms the government is proposing. For example, Make in India program. Increase in foreign investment will drive the growth and has aroused positive sentiments in the minds of the industry professionals.

   Kicked off the ambitious Startup and stand up India Movement. The government aims to fill gaps in the economy for the growth and development of startups with an aim to boost digital entrepreneurship at the grassroots and would positively impact the job market.

Corporate India is unveiling a wide variety of initiatives to hire, train and promote women in leadership positions to attain a better mix of employees and various labour reforms have also promised better prospects for the industry.

7. **Besides skills and knowledge, what kind of values you would look for in an MBA?**

   Communication, honesty and integrity, perseverance and mental toughness, team player, action oriented.

8. **How you think an MBA can contribute towards society and nation building?**

   The role of student in a developing country is huge; you can't expect a country to develop if it doesn't have literate people. These students who are studying would be working tomorrow. They would be working for public, private sectors or as an entrepreneur creating jobs for others, they would be the pillars on which the country would be standing on.

   Mahatma Gandhi once famously said "in a gentle way you can shake the whole world".

   Every person is capable in his own right as to make an impact on the society if he desires so.

   This just requires a change in attitude and shrugging off the empathetic nature that has plagued people's mindset over the years. And who better to lead and initiate this change than the people who are especially trained in the field of ethics and leaderships — The MBA students. Out of the box thinking is encouraged and inculcated among them from the very beginning and it equips them with a clear mindset free of the typical societal innuendos and stereotype mentality. So they can definitely be more proactive in working towards building a more 'inclusive' society and its betterment at the same time.

9. **What are the tips for MBA aspirants coming from relatively smaller towns and those whose medium of teaching has been Hindi?**
   - Focus on your strengths and work on your weakness.
   - Clear communication is important – Language is secondary (express yourself).
   - Have confidence.
   - Read success stories where people have done wonders in life who hail from small towns like Sir Abdul Kalam, M. Annadurai who is the programme director of Mars Orbiter Mission.
   - Prime focus on speed and accuracy is the key.

10. **What kind of preparation an aspirant should do for getting into a good B-school**.
    - Do not over/under analysing mocks.
    - Fill college forms as per your capabilities:
      - You can never predict your CAT/XAT percentile.
      - I don't care even if you're a psychic, you just can't!!
      - Do not under/overestimate yourself – Just fill the forms.
      - I am not asking you to fill every college form. But it's better to make a list of target colleges keeping your profile and work in mind.
    - Every exam is important: Most students focus just on CAT but then if you don't appear for the other exams, you would miss the opportunity of being in some really good colleges.

- With the IIMs giving so much weightage to academics, it becomes all the more important to focus on other exams like the IIFT, TISS, XAT, SNAP, NMAT and more.
- Similarly, keep working on your GK, vocabulary and decision making even though CAT doesn't have question from these.
- Fight your own Fears.

11. How should an aspirant select a good B-school?

- Faculty profile
- Cost vs ROI (Fee, placement, salary)
- Updated/latest curriculum
- Student and alumni network
- Location
- Reputation of college.

□

Command in English Language is a Must for Today's Global Business

1. **What prospects/opportunities you see for an MBA in today's scenario?**
   Taking the GMAC's 2015 survey into account, 96 percent of the employers worldwide concurred that hiring from business schools created value for their company. In the present scenario (especially in Indian context) where the economy is on the rise and the ecosystem is favorable for business expansions, the MBAs for sure can believe to see more "Achhey Din" i.e. "Better Days" in the coming times.

Anupam Raghuvanshi
Prerna Fellow,
IIM Lucknow
Director,
T.I.M.E. Varanasi

2. **What are the prospects for a fresh MBA in the industry especially banking industry both in public and private sector?**
   Tremendous opportunities. The Reserve Bank of India has planned to expand banking to nearly 70 percent of the villages (the present is roughly 7 percent) by the year 2020. This 10-fold increase directly means more job opportunities for business graduates.

3. **What are the qualities you look in a student when you prepare them for competitive exams?**
   The students coming to us are from all walks of life and diverse degree backgrounds. In B and C class towns the challenge is more due to the students being rustic on the required professional standards of personality and communication. Still a student with great integrity, aspiration value and an incessant ability to learn is what I believe may win him the race.

4. **How a student should prepare for written tests like CAT MAT?**
   Any aptitude test is more of a leveler. One's degree background and academic competence isn't something that should intimidate the candidate alone. A well-planned practice of basics and concepts followed by the all India mock tests could just be okay almost for anyone. Being regular for the classes and clearing doubts however is something that is a student's prerogative.

5. **How a student should prepare for GD or case analysis?**
   The preparation per-se shouldn't be treated as a post CAT exercise. Content development and communication skills both require incessant practice in the long run. Right from day one of his preparation, a student should be aware of the world around and must practice that through group discussions. A good way of doing this is through case studies as these give them a better platform to develop analytical skills along with content and communication. Since this is a group exercise and requires a professional environment, the training institute plays an important role.

6. **What are the tips for success in PI?**

A student must plan his career. You can't just focus on language and communication alone. There should be enough things in your CV for an interviewer to be genuinely interested in you. A student must focus on his extra and co-curricular activities along with academics. Also it is very important for students to know the world around them. There used to be a time when one's knowledge alone use to bring laurels to a person. Today people also check your level of information and awareness and your ability to deliberate your opinion based on them.

7. **Besides skills and knowledge, what kind of values you would look for in an MBA?**
   The quest of an MBA should be the quest for a leadership position. The bigger question is How fast can you climb the corporate ladder enough and lead the way? Now this simply means that integrity, humility, sincerity and a sense of responsibility is what these positions in future would basically require.
8. **How you think an MBA can contribute towards society and nation building?**
   As future business leaders and decision makers that would affect the lives of many, an MBA has more roles to play than what is perceived: wealth creation, better system, operation and smooth business process also help facilitate the life of a common man. The onus for all these certainly falls back on the shoulders of an MBA who would be somewhere playing his part. Also better business leaders would ensure better growth thereby creating bigger opportunity of employment and distribution of wealth through business process.
9. **What are the tips for MBA aspirants coming from relatively smaller towns and those whose medium of teaching has been Hindi?**

Any student of today must focus on content, concept and expression. The command on English is the key to survive the global business ecosystem and to be a part of it. Reading is something that should be made a daily affair. A regular reading of newspapers and magazine articles help build a command on the language on the whole. Fluency comes when one practice speaking. The students must make a cohort and practice speaking as much as possible to gain confidence. Most students hesitate due to lack of practice alone and eventually fail in personality rounds.

10. What kind of preparation an aspirant should do for getting into a good B-school?

Get a good score in exams like CAT. Be a consistent reader, read anything and everything that comes your way. Speak out often. Be a part of discussion groups, stay informed and be aware of all that is making news around you. That should be enough to get into a B-school of your choice.

11. How should an aspirant select a good B-school?

The claims of B-schools are getting higher by the day and the choices multiplying each year. The mushrooming of new B-schools is adding more to the plight of an already confused lot of students at large. The students must look at the following before locking on with their choices:

1. Age of the institute
2. Faculty qualification and research
3. Internship opportunities
4. Industry affiliations
5. Profiles of guest faculty and corporate people
6. Placement support and companies visiting campus.
7. Alumni network.

□

Data Analysis Skills and Interpersonal Skills form Two Key Areas in Today's Business

1. **What prospects/opportunities you see for an MBA in today's scenario?**

Mr. Jitender Sharma
Senior Librarian and Co-Editor – *Jaipuria International Journal of Management Research,* Jaipuria Institute of Management, Noida

   After the financial recession of 2008, Indian economy is again booming. Efforts by the Government of India for the growth and development of manufacturing sector in addition to services sector have resulted in tremendous potential for qualified professionals. Financial services are growing at a great pace. There is lot of scope for everyone in the financial services industry. Hence, there are much better prospects available for doing MBA in today's scenario.

2. **What are the prospects for a fresh MBA in the industry?**

   MBA degree has got worldwide fame and recognition. MBA fresher can expect to get various entry level managerial positions depending upon their specialization including managerial trainee in HR, finance, marketing, sales, business analytics and so on. One may even get directly manager position depending upon his skills.

3. **What are the qualities you look in an MBA when you go for recruitments?**
   Recruiters will look for good communication skills, team player, leadership skills, problem solving skills and strategic thinking skills in a candidate while recruiting.
4. **What specific things an MBA should do to make a sound career in industry while studying?**
   An MBA student should focus on basics of industry as without strong basic knowledge he will not move far. He should develop key skills like team building and leadership qualities. He must be open to ideas and should be a patience listener. Learning data analysis tools will help him in decision making.
5. **How an MBA should groom himself/herself for a better career path after joining industry.**
   An MBA should have an entrepreneurial mindset, should develop keen observation capabilities to identify opportunities and convert them to business. He should develop multi-skills and cross-functional exposure as employers look for people who can quickly adapt to roles provided by organizations. Developing interpersonal skills and use of data analysis tools in decision making will help a student in making sound career in industry. He should accept criticism as learning and develop positive attitude.
6. **How is industry looking up for future, say next 5 years?**
   Industry is bullish about the future. Demand for

qualified MBA professionals will grow in coming years as large multinational corporations are setting up their manufacturing base in India and they will require qualified professionals. Also, India as a market is quite attractive and has great potential which is attracting lot of foreign direct investment (FDI), hence future is very positive for industrial growth in India.

7 **Besides Skills and knowledge, what kind of values you would look for in an MBA?**

Besides the essential skills and knowledge, other values required for an MBA are quality to remain focused and committed, good communicator, creative skills, decision making skills, entrepreneurial mindset, disciplined, ethical in conduct and a team leader among others.

8. **How You think an MBA can contribute towards society and nation building?**

MBA students are taught to develop out of the box thinking helping them to have a clear mind set free of the typical stereotype societal mentality. They can be more proactive in building a more 'inclusive' society and its betterment. Through their entrepreneurial mindset they can generate employment opportunities for unprivileged sections of the society. They can help in improving operations and supply chain and developing and providing markets access to the rural people who find difficult to get market to sell their products and are exploited by middlemen. MBAs with their knowledge and skills can be of immense benefits in improving our society and hence nation building.

9. **What are the tips for MBA aspirants coming from relatively smaller towns and those whose medium of teaching has been Hindi?**

This is a myth that students from smaller towns

and studying in Hindi medium can't compete with students from cities and learning in English medium highly prestigious schools. Students need to concentrate on their basics. They should inculcate reading newspapers especially business newspapers in depth. They should work on developing their communication skills and interpersonal skills. Best way to do this is to speak in front of mirror regularly and try to improve upon your shortcomings. Make your weaknesses as your strength. Honestly speaking, the great potential to succeed for MBA is in rural areas only which are untapped markets with great potential. You may opt for a rural posting and there will you succeed more unlike an English speaking convent educated person who will not be able to adjust to rural culture easily. You need to work with a clear goal and strategy in mind and do not get distracted with other attractions that a city life offers.

10. **What kind of preparation an aspirant should do for getting into a good B School?**

Getting to a good B-school is at least a three tier process. It requires qualifying written tests with good score, going through group discussion process followed by personal interviews. You need to start well in advance preparing for admission tests like CAT, MAT, C-MAT and so on. You need to work on your basics very hard. Habit of reading newspapers in depth will help you in developing good general knowledge and right inputs for your group discussions and personal interviews. Find out the syllabus of entrance exam and start preparing at least one year in advance. You may take the help of previous year questions papers to see what type of questions is asked in the exams. You have to perfect time management skills. Further you need to work on developing communication skills. You have to handle group discussion very carefully. Never try to impose your point of view on others during GD process. You need to put your point of views in clear and precise manner but at the same time listen to what others are saying. You need to learn to take initiative in starting a discussion and get involved in discussions. Put forward your views and politely mention your difference of opinion if any from other participants views. Also you should participate in extra-curricular activities at school level and highlight the achievements during personal interviews. During personal interviews, you must understand that interviewer will judge you in those five-ten minutes based upon your attitude, communication skills and your approach to answer a question. Hence, you should answer in clear, precise and calculated manner that reflects your approach as a learner, team player and problem solver rather than a self centered, egoistic person.

11. How should an aspirant select a good b school??

Keep a regular eye on when the admission process is starting in good b-schools. Appear for the entrance exams. First of all, identify the good b-school which you want to apply well in advance. Do not go by false claims or full page advertisements by B-schools. You need to verify the facts mentioned on their websites or in their advertisements. You need to check if the institute is approved and recognized by competent authorities. Are all approvals in place? Check the placement record of the B-school and if possible, find and talk to alumni of that B-school. Find out the availability of faculty and facilities in the B-school. If possible, make a personal visit to the B-school and talk to students studying in that B-school.

□

Annenure 1
Some Important Websites Related to Placement

1 Indian Banking Association
http://www.iba.org.in/
2 India Brand Equity Foundation
http://www.ibef.org/
3 The Securities and Exchange Board of India
http://www.sebi.com/
4 Silicon India http://www.siliconindia.com/
5 RBI https://www.rbi.org.in/
6 Glassdoor https://www.glassdoor.co.in
7 Quora India https://www.quora.com/
8 Placement Pappers
http://placementpapers.net/helpingroot/home
9 India Bix http://www.indiabix.com/placement-papers/companies/
10 All India Association of Industries
http://www.aiaiindia.com/
11 Retailers Association of India
http://www.rai.net.in/
12 Cellular Operators Association of India
http://www.coai.com//

Annenure 2
Some Important Websites Related to Rankings

NRHDN-Peoples Matters
https://www.peoplematters.in/article/2015/03/04/skilling/nhrdn-people-matters-b-school-ranking-data-insights-2015/10730

Business Today 2014:
http://bschools.businesstoday.in/

Career 360 - 2014 ranking
http://www.bschool.careers360.com/top-100-b-schools-in-india-2014

EduUniveral Business Schools Ranking
http://www.eduniversal-ranking.com/business-school-university-ranking-in-india.html

Outlook Magazine B-school Survey
http://www.outlookindia.com/ article/indias-best-bschools-in-2015/ 295392

Business World Magazine
http://www.businessworld.in/article/B-School -Rankings-2015/08-12-2015-89117/

CSR-GHRDC survey available up to 2014
http://ghrdc.org/website/B-SchoolSurvey/2014/Reports.html

MBA Universe National Institutional Ranking
http://www.mbauniverse.com/ bschool ranking2015/b-school-rankings.php

Framework https://www.nirfindia.org/Home

Annenure 3
Curriculum Vitae

Name: Email: Mobile:
Address:
Date of Birth:

SUMMER INTERNSHIP

- Ratnagiri Gas and Power Private Ltd., Noida May'14-June'14
- Review on Financial Statements and Business Plan of Ratnagiri Gas and Power Private Ltd.
- Analyzed the financial position of the company for the year 2010-11, 2011-12 and 2012-13
- Evaluated the business plan and suggested measures for improvement

PROFESSIONAL EXPERIENCE

- The Park Hotel (APJ Group) Jun'08-0ct'08
- Coordinated and managed catering operations to assure quality services
- Oversee transportation and set-up activities to ensure successful onboard catering

ACADEMIC QUALIFICATIONS

- PGDM (Pursuing), Finance, XXX Institute of Management, XXX, 2015, 9.45/10
- B. Com (Honours), Maharaja Agrasen College, University of Delhi, 2013, 65.94%
- Higher Secondary Schooling, Vishwa Bharati Public School, Noida, 2010, 80.80%
- Secondary Schooling, Vishwa Bharati Public School, Noida, 2008, 84.80%

CERTIFICATIONS

- Six Sigma Green Belt from KPMG, 2015

ADDITIONAL PROJECTS

- Comparison of Ratios at Tata Steel Ltd. And Jindal Steel Ltd. Aug'13
- Analyzed the liquidity ratios and solvency ratios of Tata Steel Ltd. and Jindal Steel & Power Ltd.

ACHIEVEMENTS

- Top scorer in Academics, Batch 2013-15, XXX Institute of Management, XXX
- Won Inter college dramatics competition in XXX Institute of Management Annual Cultural Fest
- Represented XXX Institute of Management, XXX at PHD Chambers conference

CO-CURRICULAR ACTIVITIES

- Secured first position in NukkadNatak (AROHAN) in UDAAN 2013
- Coordinator of Dramatics Club.
- Active member of Research Cell and Finance Club.

INTERESTS

- Reading Novels
- Listening to Music
- Cooking

Annenure 4
Some Leading Business Schools of the Country

No.	Institute	State
1.	IIM, Ahmedabad	Gujarat
2.	IIM, Calcutta	West Bengal
3.	XLRI, Jamshedpur	Jharkhand
4.	SPJIMR, Mumbai	Maharashtra
5.	MDI, Gurgaon	Haryana
6.	FMS, Delhi	Delhi
7.	IIM, Kozhikode	Kerala
8.	IIM, Indore	Madhya Pradesh
9.	IMI, Delhi	Delhi
10.	IIFT, Delhi	Delhi
11.	NMIMS, Mumbai	Maharashtra
12.	NITIE, Mumbai	Maharashtra
13.	IMT, Ghaziabad	Uttar Pradesh
14.	XIM, Bhubaneswar	Odisha
15.	SIBM, Pune	Maharashtra
16.	VGSoM, IIT Kharagpur	West Bengal
17.	DMS, IIT Delhi	Delhi
18.	TAPMI, Manipal	Karnataka
19.	IIM, Shillong	Meghalaya
20.	BIMTECH, Gr Noida	Uttar Pradesh
21.	SJMSOM, IIT Bombay	Maharashtra
22.	IRMA, Anand	Gujarat
23.	SCMHRD, Pune	Maharashtra
24.	Institute of Management, Nirma University	Gujarat
25.	Goa Institute of Management	Goa
26.	JBIMS,	Mumbai

27. LN Welingkar Institute of Management, Mumbai
28. Lal Bahadur Shastri Institute of Management, Delhi — Delhi
29. KJ Somaiya Institute of Management, Mumbai — Maharashtra
30. MANAGE, Hyderabad — Telangana
31. SIMSREE, Mumbai — Maharashtra
32. Department of Management Studies, IIS, Bangalore — Karnataka
33. Department of Management Studies, NIT Tiruchirappalli — Tamil Nadu
34. BIM, Tiruchirappalli — Tamil Nadu
35. AIMS School of Business — Karnataka
36. Asia-Pacific Institute of Management, Delhi — Delhi
37. LIBA, — Chennai
38. Indian Institute of Management, Ranchi — Jharkhand
39. PSG Institute of Management, Coimbatore — Tamil Nadu
40. IISWBM, Kolkata — West Bengal
41. ITM, Navi Mumbai — Maharashtra
42. Rajagiri Centre for Business Studies, Kochi — Kerala
43. Amity Business School, Noida — Uttar Pradesh
44. Jaipuria Institute of Management, Noida/Lucknow, — Uttar Pradesh
45. Institute for Financial Management and Research — Andhra Pradesh
46. School of Management, KIIT University — Odisha
47. IMT, Nagpur — Maharashtra
48. BIMM, Pune — Maharashtra
49. XIME, Bangalore — Karnataka
50. SCMS Cochin School of Business — Kerala

Annenure 5
Important Coaching Institutions of the Country

1. IMS Learning Centre
2. Jamboree Education
3. Achiever's Academy
4. Ascent Education
5. Brilliant Tutorials
6. Bulls Eye
7. BYJU's CAT Classes
8. Career Forum
9. Career Launcher
10. Career Plan
11. CET Tutorials
12. Competitive Careers
13. Endeavor Careers
14. Erudite
15. Excel Management Foundation
16. Expert Education
17. Foundation Studies for Management
18. KITS
19. Magnus Institute
20. Matrix Academy
21. Prism Centre for Education
22. PT Education
23. Real Business Education
24. Sachdeva College
25. SKD Educational Consultant

26. TIME (Triumphant Institute of Management Education)
27. Vidyamandir
28. Vidyasagr Classes

Annenure 6
Important Counselling Websites

1. www.shiksha.com
2. www.pagalguy.com
3. www.minglebox.com/
4. www.htcampus.com
5. www.jagranjosh.com/
6. www.careerlauncher.com/
7. TCYonline - A lot of free sample tests available online
8. TestFunda - provides CAT preparation material in versions - print, online, CD and android
9. Alchemist - classroom as well as online prep (online discussion, videos, pdf files, e-books)
10. http://online.2iim.com/
11. MBAuniverse.com
12. Career Line Education
13. www.hitbulleye.com
14. www.tcyonline.com/
15. www.wisdom24x7.com/
16. www.prep.youth4work.com/Management
17. MBAcrystalball - Best for GMAT preparation online
18. Mindworkzz - webinar lectures by 11M alumni, Arun Sharma

Annenure 7
Some Useful Aps

1. Pagalguy
2. CAT Entrance
3. Testfunda.com
4. Career Launcher
5. CMAT
6. IIM CAT Test Prep
7. Bulls Eyes
8. Jagran Josh
9. Mingalbox